SAYING HELLO;
WAVING GOODBYE

SAYING HELLO;
WAVING GOODBYE

◆

To This Wonderful Thing Called Life

Nancy M. Hoch

ASJA Press

New York Lincoln Shanghai

SAYING HELLO; WAVING GOODBYE
To This Wonderful Thing Called Life

ASJA Press
an imprint of iUniverse, Inc.

iUniverse books may be ordered through booksellers or by contacting:

iUniverse
2021 Pine Lake Road, Suite 100
Lincoln, NE 68512
www.iuniverse.com
1-800-Authors (1-800-288-4677)

ISBN-13: 978-0-595-42018-6
ISBN-10: 0-595-42018-4

Printed in the United States of America

DEDICATED TO

Mother & Dad,

my dear Dean,

& our five sons,

& their wonderful families

A TIME FOR ALL THINGS

Centuries before the Meridian of Time, Ecclesiastes, the Preacher of the Old Testament, said:

> "To every thing there is a season, and a time to every purpose under the heaven:
> A time to be born, and a time to die ...
> A time to weep, and a time to laugh ..."

To which we might add:

> A time to "*Say Hello*" and a time to "*Wave Goodbye*."

Contents

Acknowledgments

Special thanks to my sister, Mary, and my good friends, Lynn Leonard and Flos Rexroat, for reading the drafts of this book. Also Dr. Susan Swetnam of the English Department at Idaho State University for her great job of editing, and Eddie Hale at ISU for her outstanding technical assistance with the manuscript.

I must also thank my dear "partner in crime," and husband, Dean, for his support and encouragement, and my family for the inspiration behind so many of the essays and vignettes (or "vinaigrettes," as Dean calls 'em).

Introduction

SAYING "HELLO"

"Hi. What's your name?"

Kellie, our darling, little six-year-old, is nattily dressed in play clothes, her silky blond pony tail bouncing as she runs about.

Her question is posed to a boy who replies, "I'm Brandon."

Brandon looks just a trifle older and wiser than Kellie.

The two nonchalantly begin to climb and play on the big, purple and pink jungle gym with its flexible, rubber bridge, metal bars, and huge, spinable tic-tac-toe blocks. On this warm, languid summer evening, other children are already having fun in the pleasant setting of the local park.

Happy to volunteer to take our granddaughter, Kellie, for a few hours of fun, I observe all the activity from my seat on a nearby park bench. I feel the heat of the sun on my face, and occasionally glance up at the bird's-egg-blue sky, cottony white clouds, and the infinite shades of green in the tall trees.

Thoughts travel gently on the pathways of my mind as I watch Kellie.

I, along with the other adults, chuckle as we see a darling three-year-old boy, with droopy pants, excitedly splash in the water of the drinking fountain, creating the inevitable mud puddle beneath.

Kellie and Brandon, meanwhile, are continuing in their abandonment of running, chasing, climbing, and flying down the slides time after time.

Giggles ensue. A occasional bump, then a child cries and wails. The seemingly insatiable tears are wiped away by a caring someone, and the jolly play resumes.

All too soon, the rich, gold and vermillion colors of the summer sunlight begin to fade, and the day comes to its inevitable close.

Brandon's mother beckons. He waves "Goodbye" to Kellie who reluctantly relinquishes her tenuous hold on this brief but warm friendship.

"It's time to go," I tell Kellie.

"But I want to stay," she says, tears brimming in her bright, blue eyes.

"It's time," I reply, taking her hand in mine.

Kellie realizes she has no choice but to go.

The park empties and, as we leave, I think how much like our lives is this lovely day.

From the time we say "Hello" to the world, until it is time to "Wave Good-bye," we all share in the many relationships, the strivings and accomplishments, the learning and growing, the bumps and tears, and the fun and excitement of it all, until, inevitably, the sunlight fades, and it is time to go.

Since I am closer to the "Waving Goodbye" part of this whole, wonderful process, the following vignettes and essays are written to capture snatches of my own day at the park. I do this with the hope that others might find meaning in them, as they experience their own turn on this wonderful playground called life.

A TIME OF
BEGINNINGS

I REMEMBER PAPA

Because I have five sons, who are now all fathers themselves, I decided one day to record some memories of my own father, in the hopes a thought or two might be an influence for good as they raise their own daughters and sons. Each dad, of course, is a unique individual, and each has his own strengths and weaknesses, but it's important that each thinks now and then of the kind of legacy he will leave his own children.

With that thought in mind, this little piece reflects the legacy my father left his family when he died.

Back in the 1940's, there was a popular movie called, "I Remember Mama."

Certainly I do remember my Mama, or "Mum," as I called her. She was dear to me and taught me much. For the most part, she was patient, taking time to sing to me and listen to me read my first Dick and Jane books to her, but occasionally she'd get a switch after me for running away down the street when I was a little tyke. She was also one never to take any "lip," and all three of her children respected and loved her.

It was "Papa," however, or Daddy, or Dad, as we called him, who had the most influence on my life. Perhaps it was the father/daughter thing—fathers shaping so much of their daughters' success in life—and in their relationships with other men in their lives, especially in the success of their own marriages. Psychologists tell us over and over that much of a balanced outlook on life derives from a girl's relationship with her father, and a boy's with his mother, and of the importance of both a male and a female figure in the home.

I've tried, often, to analyze just how my father influenced my own life so greatly.

My earliest memories are those of him reading to me as I sat on his lap. I wrote a whole story about the evening he taught me not to fear a thunderstorm. I was about six at the time.

It was fun to hear him joke around and tell funny stories. Though a serious man, I know he put forth an extra effort to make our home a happy one. He also took the time to make me feel important and loved.

I remember thinking of him as a handsome man, about five feet, ten inches tall, with dark hair, blue eyes, a bit on the heavy side, with a quick smile and a pleasant countenance. He liked to make me and others laugh at every opportunity.

I wrote in my personal life story that Dad and I took frequent walks together, but, as I think back, it was only a handful of times that we walked together around Edinboro, Pennsylvania, the little college/resort town where I grew up. Those walks made a big impression on me and are among my most cherished memories.

Perhaps this is because I appreciated my dad taking the time to do this. Perhaps it was because of the unhurried nature of the walks—picking up leaves in the fall and studying rocks that looked like fossils. Perhaps it was talking together and sharing thoughts about this and that. Perhaps it was because I looked up to my dad and loved him so much.

Sometimes we would take the camera, and Dad would show me how to take photos. We would pick up walking sticks to help us over rough terrain.

One special winter evening, we walked though the falling snow, having the fun of seeing it glitter against the street lights. Our destination was the little jewelry store on Erie Street in Edinboro where we stopped to select a pearl necklace for Mother for Christmas.

Dad sometimes recited poetry as we walked, and I remember to this day lines from the Rubyiat of Omar Khyyam, Gray's Elegy Written in a Country Church-Yard, The Village Blacksmith, The Highwayman, Barbara Fritchie, and others.

He told me stories of his own mother that he had loved so much who died when he was only fourteen years old—how she longed for her homeland in Ireland, and how she loved him. Knowing she was dying, he bought her a record of one of her favorite songs.

As an adult, Dad was a hard-working man who would rather be with his family than anywhere else. When I was only five, I remember meeting him at the bus stop as he came home from work, and he would take me now and then to the drug store for a cherry soda. I was in seventh heaven.

It must be said that Dad did have a violent temper. One day he was so angry with my sister when she was young that he chased her up the stairs and into her room. She darted under the bed, and he dove right in after her. Being small, she was able to extricate herself quickly on the other side. Dad, however, managed to catch the seat of his pants on the protruding bed springs, and the episode, fortunately, broke down into humor. Lucky for my sister!

It was definitely not a humorous situation, however, when my brother, Bob, as a teenager, came home late one night—much later than his curfew allowed. He made the matter worse by saying something sassy. My father, sad to say, hit Bob in the face with his fist and knocked him across the room—a memory our family would all just as soon forget.

Gratefully, these occasions were rare, and my mother did her best to keep things on an even keel, helping to avert or subdue these occasional outbursts.

My dad had been raised in a home with far too much corporal punishment and far too many harsh words. He had vowed his own home would never be like that. Most of the time he kept that vow, and I, being the last of the litter, never experienced the worst of his wrath. Thank heaven, he had learned to keep it under control by that time, for which I am grateful.

Only once, when I was late coming home as a teenager, did he "cloud up and rain down all over," as he used to say from time to time. I'll never forget the anger in his face when I entered the back door of the house. Therefore, knowing the temper he had and respecting him as my father, I walked a careful line to stay in his good graces.

When I was in high school, Dad was interested enough in my studies to make the valiant attempt to learn Spanish along with me. I laughed when he would purposely say, "ab-dobe" instead of "adobe." He also jokingly mis-pronounced Agamemnon, when I was studying Greek history. His version was something like "Aga-mem-won." We had lots of laughs as he would repeat these words over and over just for the fun of it.

Also in junior high and high school, Dad enjoyed much of the same music I enjoyed. We both liked Classical, but he also danced around our living room to the tunes of the time. When traveling with his job, if he liked something on the "hit parade," he would swing into a music store, buy a 45 rpm record, and bring it home for the family to enjoy.

He and Mother both loved to dance and were the hit of any evening of ball-room dancing. They waltzed divinely, and Dad taught me to love to dance as well. One night when Mother wasn't feeling well, he took me to Syria Mosque in Pittsburgh to a lovely evening affair. Though only ten at the time, I felt so honored to be his dancing partner. He also took me there another evening to see Nat King Cole perform. What sweet memories for a young girl to recall.

I feel so terribly sorry for girls who are abused by their fathers, and I will be eternally grateful my father was not that kind of monster.

As I became a young woman, Dad never actually told me what he and my Mother expected of me in my behavior on dates. Mother minced no words on the subject, but it was Dad who said, "If you slip, and something goes terribly wrong, always remember that your place is here at home."

I knew what he meant, but I made up my mind I would do everything in my power never to have to take him up on that kind and generous offer.

No doubt the most important thing about being a father is simply taking the time to show that you care and to tell a child often that you do. It's the little day-to-day things that mean so very much and rarely, if ever, the material things. Rather, it's the little acts of love that let children know they are dear and special.

That, after all, is how all of us hope we will be remembered—struggling to do our best, knowing we're far from perfect, but striving daily to carry on, trying to set a good example, and enduring to the end.

With gratitude in my heart, that's just the way "I remember Papa."

JUST WAIT IT OUT

"It's hard to beat Pennsylvania for lightning storms," my dad said matter-of-factly.

The calmness in his voice did not match the fear building in my six-year-old heart. My eyes darted about the room, as the sky suddenly went black and the wind increased in intensity.

"Hurry, Bob, close the windows," my mother called.

As he did so, the first great rumble of thunder split the quiet sounds of the summer night. The power of it shook our house from roof to foundation.

I screamed and flew to my mother's arms for safety.

"It's okay," she said, trying to comfort my fears.

Seconds later, an immense flash of lightning illuminated the interior of the house, making bright daylight out of the ever-darkening sky.

I ran from her arms to those of my father as he settled himself in the big, over-stuffed chair near our living room window.

"Don't be afraid, honey," he said, stroking my braided, brown hair. "Learn to respect storms, but don't be afraid of them. It can be thrilling to watch nature put on her electrical display. Just wait it out, and pretty soon everything will be calm again."

I pressed closer to his big, warm chest, cuddling as deeply as I could into his lap, feeling the firm, yet gentle strength of his arms.

Another great burst of thunder overshadowed all other sounds. Jagged lightning once again split the nighttime sky.

"I'm scared," I whimpered, shuddering under the impact.

"Once when I was a young man," my dad said, "I was right in the middle of a storm ten times bigger than this one."

Just hearing his thoughts distracted me, the comfort of his arms continuing to reassure me. He seemed so sure of himself, and his words made me feel that, because he was near, nothing could bring harm to me.

"I was sailing on a huge troop ship to France to fight in a big war," he continued. "A great storm at sea began to develop one afternoon, two days out of our port in England. Everyone hurried below decks to get out of the wind and rain.

But I decided to crawl up on a huge pile of barracks bags, under the shelter of an upper deck. There, I was able to watch the boiling ocean and experience the thrill of my young life. The sky and ocean were both a deep, dark gray. The waves were like mountains crashing over the decks of the ship, and the wind was fierce, with a shrieking sound that never let up. I burrowed among the bags, amazed at the power of nature, marveling that the big ship could stay afloat."

Even as a child, I could begin to see the majesty of the storm through his eyes. This was because of the images his words created so vividly in my mind.

"Finally it was all over," he said, "and at dusk I went below to my bunk. I had missed mess (which was our dinner), but it was worth it."

Another boom of thunder, and our living room once again alternated from darkness to brightness and to darkness once again.

"The thunder and lighting are putting on their show," Dad said, as the Eastern summer storm gradually spent itself.

With his words, I began to have an early appreciation of the magnificence of nature's fury and of the respite that comes once a storm is over. We sat there together until the storm subsided. Then, contented and happy, I returned to my play.

Since that day I no longer fear a storm. I respect its power and one rarely occurs but what I think of that day when my father taught me how to view nature—and life, too—without dread.

As I grew, Dad sometimes commented that he felt like a failure. He never earned a degree nor a big amount of money. He was not recognized by the world for any of his achievements. He was simply a family man.

However, to me he was a hero, and how to deal with the fear of a storm was just one of the many lessons he taught me.

Other lessons involved how to show kindness toward those less fortunate and those who saw the world differently than I did. I watched as he listened with courtesy to all kinds and types of people, including, for example, his lively conversations with people such as the Italian repairman who came often to our home and who spoke with such a heavy accent. Dad joked and had a good time with everyone.

On a more serious note, I remember when Dad served as the school board president long ago in our small college town. It fell to him to be the one to dismiss Mr. Jamison (name changed), the elementary principal who, it was learned, was enticing and abusing a number of the little boys in the school. My father expressed only sorrow to our family for this man he believed was otherwise such a fine individual. He said, "None of us are perfect, and we need to be kind to others, especially in their most extreme and difficult circumstances."

Dad showed me how to go forward with fortitude in the face of adversity. Knowing he had severe heart problems, he once showed me, when I was about twelve and we were traveling together, how to reach over, turn off the key, and steer the car to the edge of the road, should he ever slump over at the wheel.

With his great sense of humor, he taught me how to laugh at my own foibles and how to help others laugh, especially in times of trial and difficulty. I marveled at his ability, even at somber funeral homes, to make people laugh. He did this in such a kindly, caring way that the spirits of those who were grieving were gently lifted.

He also taught me how to care for those in need. At his own funeral, young couples, and students, and those who were "down and out," as Dad sometimes called them, revealed after the service how my father had often pressed money into their hands saying, "Have a dinner on me … or use this for some books … or here's a little something to tide you over." What a comforting revelation these comments were to our family.

My father also showed me how to use careful thought and wisdom in making those decisions that would have the greatest impact on my life. When I casually dated a young man of another race for a short time, my Dad sat down with me and said, "Nancy, you're wise enough to know that interracial and interfaith marriages can and often do work out just fine. However, think about the fact that marriage is no easy business—even when the people involved are of the same race and the same faith. The more alike you are, the greater the odds are that you'll have success. I know you will weigh many factors before making all the important decisions in your life. Do rest assured that your mother and I may offer words of caution before any of our children marry, but once they do, we've made a pact to keep our mouths shut."

I had every confidence that my father would support me in whatever my final decisions might be—and he did.

I was also grateful for the confidence he built into me and my sister long before the women's movement was in full swing. He often said, "Nancy, you can do anything you want to do … be anything you want to be. Think about becoming a doctor. You have the brains for it … or be a great writer, or a college professor and help shape people's lives. Do what makes you happiest and gives you the greatest fulfillment."

Finally, when my father died, he taught me what leaving a worthwhile legacy is all about. Throughout my life, his words have come forcefully to mind whenever thunder and lightning of one kind or another rend my world.

"There will be plenty of storms in your life, honey," he often said. "Have respect for them, but don't be afraid of them either. Just wait it out and, before you know it, everything will be calm once again."

MOVIES, MEMORIES, and MORE

"Would you like to read *The Hidden Hand*?" she'd ask, "or maybe *Betty Zane* or *The Spirit of the Border* by Zane Grey?" Whatever book we happened to choose, she would be the first to curl up in one of the overstuffed chairs beside our flagstone fireplace and point for me to sit nearby.

That cozy fireplace was special to both of us because our Mother and Dad had built it into the living room wall of our hundred-year-old home in Edinboro, the quiet little resort and college town where our family lived in Northwestern Pennsylvania. The two of them had handpicked the stones on the shore of Lake Erie twenty miles to the north.

Thirteen years younger than my sister, Mary, I felt it an honor to sit in a chair close to hers where we would spend hours reading, often with the spicy smell of Mother's delicious gingerbread or others of her culinary delights wafting through the house.

"I'll read first," she'd say, and she read very well. At age 23, it was obvious she could read much better than I at age ten. However, she was patient with me, and I loved the experience of sharing this time with her. Because of it, I maintained a love of reading throughout my life. Besides, this proved to be a great time for sister bonding.

Our relationship hadn't started out all that idyllic, however.

"Do I have to babysit her *again*?" Mary would complain to our mother. "She cries over anything; she's a pain in the neck."

It was true. I did fuss and cry a lot (or so I was later told), definitely cramping my teenage sister's style. Our poor mother couldn't take me any place with my bawling, and so Sis was called upon much too often, she believed, to babysit.

As I grew, I came to learn I was the proverbial mistake, albeit my mother told me it was a good mistake. She and my dad were nearly forty when I made my appearance. My only brother, Bob—nine at the time—managed to tolerate me. He even took me for rides on the handlebars of his old bike when I was about five

11

or six. My only sister, meanwhile, understandably could have wished at times that I had never come along.

My mother thought her early pregnancy symptoms were the "change of life," as she called it. But it wasn't the "change of life." It was a whole other and very dramatic change for her—*me*! And I wasn't all that welcome to her or to the rest of the family for that matter. What a way to enter the world—unwanted and unloved. Just kidding—even though there was an element of truth in the matter.

Nevertheless, exercising all my charm (at least after the bawling days), I think I managed to overcome all that and, as the years passed, I did my best to set things right by working my way into everyone's hearts—at least that's what I was told, as the years went by and my place in the family became established. Over time they all told me how much they loved me, and I knew the words were sincere. Let me add that it was a bit uphill at times, however, for all of us.

My sister, Mary, married a wonderful guy named Ken Croney when she was twenty, and I only seven. A returned World War II serviceman, I thought Ken was very handsome, especially when I first saw him in his Air Force uniform.

As the years passed, Ken took Mary to Hawaii, and Texas, and New Jersey, and Seattle with his work as an engineer for Bell Laboratories. However, he always saw to it that she got home to Pennsylvania for several weeks every summer, and those weeks did much to build our love and relationship as sisters … and as the only two girls in the family.

On summer trips with our parents from Pittsburgh to Atlantic City or Washington, D.C., Mary would teach me all the hit songs of the day. Looking back, I know I had a remarkable memory for one so young. I remembered the lyrics of those songs my entire life and in later years often sang them on trips with my own family. Of course, the learning of them took place in those wonderful days when songs were delightfully singable and the lyrics worth remembering—tunes such as "Oh, you beautiful doll," "Paper doll," "Unforgettable," "Make Believe," "I'll Be Seeing You," "Old Man River," "If I Loved You," and many of the hits from "South Pacific," "Oklahoma," "The King and I," and on, and on.

When I was at the awkward age of 12, Mary took me on a bus trip, just the two of us, from Edinboro two hours south to Pittsburgh, where both of us and our brother, Bob, had been born. Mary and I spent two super fun days there together.

On the way, we had to change buses just over the state line in Youngstown, Ohio. Being tall and gangly for my age, when the bus pulled into the station, I grabbed my suitcase and, acting the fool, stepped down to exit the bus. On that first step I gingerly jumped up just for the fun of it, and in so doing cracked the top of my head on the doorway of the bus. Seeing stars from the pain, I let go of my suitcase which bounced down the remaining steps, landing on the pavement. It broke open, and all my clothing, including my underwear fell on the ground, exposing everything in its entirety "to the rude gaze of the barbarous multitude," a colorful expression attributed to Somerset Maugham.

Needless to say, I was one embarrassed young lady.

Mary quickly said, "Hey, you dumb kid. What in heaven's name are you doing?"

Actually, I don't really remember her saying anything, only laughing her head off and helping me scoop everything up so we could go into the depot before heading on to Pittsburgh once again. I was certain every eye at the depot was on me. Now, even though we still laugh about the episode, I swear my poor head has never been right since. It provides an excuse, I say, for some occasional aberrant behavior. My husband laughingly adds, "Amen," and/or "I'm glad you have an excuse."

After getting settled in our hotel room, Mary and I went to two movies that first evening. One was Marlon Brando in *Viva Zapata*, and I forget the other. The next day we went to three more shows at different theaters in the downtown area. One was *The Merry Widow*; another, Elvis Presley's first film, and a third, Anthony Perkins in *Psycho*. Legitimately, there are people who might say the two of *us* were "psycho."

I still chuckle over two sisters seeing five movies in a day and a half, in between a little shopping here and there in Pittsburgh's big department stores. Only two silly sisters would have done such a thing, I suppose. Nevertheless, Mary loved it, and so did I.

While in Edinboro, we often attended the Best Theater. Whether or not one considered it the "best" in town, it was the only one, and it served the college community as well as the large number of farmers and laborers in the area.

I remember one evening when the film version of Shakespeare's "Henry V" was playing. My father happened to be standing near the entrance when he noticed a burly, rough-hewn man exiting just about a half hour after the film began.

Dad said, "Don't you like the movie?" to which the man replied, "Naw, no point to it."

Enough said about the "best" of some of the folks who attended the Best.

As a family we took in just about every new film that played at this theater, and Mary and I enjoyed sharing many of them during her summer visits.

When I was 14, my dad took a job in Los Angeles, and he and my mother and I moved to Southern California for a couple of years. My brother had since married and remained behind with his young family in Pittsburgh.

Within months after the move, I came home one day from my ninth grade class at Washington Irving Junior High School in Glendale.

"I have a bump on my leg," I told my mother.

She had to press into the flesh to feel the rather large lump on the rear of my right leg just below the knee.

"It feels like a charley horse," she said. "Does it hurt?"

"No," I replied. "It just feels weird."

Not wasting any time, she made an appointment with a doctor, and the x-rays showed a bone tumor the size of an egg.

Dr. Wolfe, a dear old German surgeon said, "I sinc ve need to get in dere right avay and remove zis ting." I still remember his heavy accent and the shuffle of his crippled walk through the hospital corridors.

Being young, I had no clue this could portend anything serious. My dear mother, however, was sick with worry, but it was typical of her and my dad not to show their concern to me in any way. They only spoke of it later.

The surgery took three hours, and I had to spend ten days confined in a hospital bed with a metal cage protecting the healing fibula, the small bone where the tumor had attached itself. Though it had penetrated half way through the bone, the tumor was fortunately non-malignant; however the recovery was slow, and I spent several weeks on crutches.

Mary was living in Texas with Ken at the time, but she wasted no time flying to be with me and my mother and dad. On our first outing together, you can guess what the two of us chose to do—see a movie, of course. It was Jose Ferrer playing the French artist, Toulouse Lautrec, in the film *Moulin Rouge*.

After a few weeks, Mary said, "Why don't I take Nancy home with me for a while?" My parents jumped for joy at the idea. Hey, wait a minute!

They did agree, so Mary and I were off on a big Greyhound bus for the long trip to the southern tip of Texas. She and Ken lived in San Benito, near Harlingen Air Force base where Ken was working at the time. I spent a month with them in the sultry, summer Gulf heat.

What did we do? For starters we swam in the Gulf of Mexico, and I got the worst sunburn of my entire life on an overcast day at Boca Chica Beach. We read books, of course, and what else? MOVIES. We went for fun, but also for escaping from the intense heat for a few hours, and for a sharing time. One movie in particular I remember that we saw was *The Moon is Blue*. The word "virgin" was mentioned for the first time on screen, and people of the day gasped at such boldness. How times have changed.

Mary bought me a beautiful, yellow Rose Marie Reid bathing suit that summer, and I imagined myself as Esther Williams, the movie water queen, every time I wore it.

Mother, Dad, and I returned to live in Pittsburgh when I was a Sophomore in high school, and several years later Mary came home once again for my wedding. She was my maid of honor and, of course, my wedding would have been incomplete without her.

My sweet sis spent two years crocheting an elaborate bedspread as my wedding gift. The intricate piece won blue ribbons in at least a couple of state fairs, and I often look at it and think of the love it conveyed.

As the years passed, the deaths of our Father and Mother tore at both our hearts.

Mary continued to make it a point to pay a yearly visit to me and Dean and our growing family of boys in our new home in Sacramento. "Aunt Mary" established herself as an institution in the lives our five, just as she had been in my own growing up years. "Uncle Ken" took a close second in their affections.

It's said a bond exists between siblings that is deep, meaningful, and lasting. This, I believe is true. I'm grateful for Mary and all we have shared over our lifetimes. We became, and have remained, best friends.

The two of us speak only once in a great while about the day when one of us will get the "tap on the shoulder." These were the words used by Peter Marshall, former Chaplain of the United States Senate, to describe the day each of us completes our turn on earth and heads back home.

She often says, "What would we ever do without you, Nancy?" (a far cry from how she felt about me years ago).

My reply is typically, "We both know none of us is guaranteed tomorrow, and I would miss you just as much as you would miss me."

Then we just smile at each other, both understanding deep feelings. These conversations are few and far between, but we know they convey, as adequately as words can, the love we have for each other as sisters.

For both of us, our great delight as adults (after our kids were raised), became traveling to many parts of the world with our husbands, who also enjoyed each other's company. This, along with the sharing of so many blessings, particularly books, plays, concerts, and travel, the help through difficult days, our enjoyment in researching our family history together, the understanding and perspective on life and living that is ours, has meant so much.

I'm grateful the joy of having a sister was mine. I'm grateful for Mary and, though the better ones are more scarce these days than they once were, both of us are still grateful for the *MOVIES!*

THE NIGHTINGALE

Few buildings are as exquisitely beautiful as the lovely Heinz Chapel located at the heart of the University of Pittsburgh campus. My parents had taken me there often as a child, and I had marveled at its beauty, both inside and out—the sweeping lawns of manicured grass leading up to it, the intricate spires of varying heights piercing the sky, and the stained glass windows reflecting diamonds of light on the stone stillness inside.

At the time of those early visits, I never dreamed that I would one day be in a choral event—lifting my voice, along with others, in all that splendor—competing with fifteen other girls ensemble singing groups from various parts of the State of Pennsylvania.

It was my Senior year of high school, and I knew how insecure we all were in this beautiful, yet unfamiliar setting. I also felt the reassurance, however, that we, as a tight-knit group of twelve friends, had come this far in the competition.

It seemed we all knew this was a pivotal day, indeed a pivotal time in our lives and that this competition would be a part of turning each of us from girlhood to womanhood. This assurance had come, in large measure, because of a complicated man, Roger MacDougall (name changed), who was our choir and ensemble director.

Not handsome, Mac, as we called him (out of earshot) was large and rugged, an ex-Marine whose lined, 35-year-old face showed weathering beyond what one would expect from a man his age. His Scottish ancestry made you think he could march straight out of the Highlands, kilt blowing in the breeze, along with the likes of William Wallace and Robert the Bruce.

As our group waited for our call to perform, I pondered the knowledge each of us in our girls ensemble had that this man's soul burned with a love of great music, and he shared that love in a special way with his students.

Just one example was having our full chorus of a hundred or so "men and women," as he called us, attempt a two-hour performance of Handel's difficult oratorio, "Messiah," as our Christmas offering to the community. It was hardly flawless but an experience none of us would ever forget. How he could bear with a bunch of high school kids through all the grueling rehearsals, I often wondered.

17

Fact of the matter was that he *did not* bear patiently at all. In fact, he would often fly into rages and stomp about decrying our inability to give the music our all.

Nevertheless, most of us came to understand him, and none of us would be quite the same after singing under his firm and unyielding baton. In later years, I pondered the impact he had on all of us, including his sharing of books and thoughts on life. This often occurred in small groups over a Coke or hot chocolate in the local Crossroads Diner, often on wintry nights with wind and snow blowing outside the foggy windows of the place. A converted railroad car, the little restaurant was a popular gathering place not far from our school.

Mac would discuss the short stories of Somerset Maugham and the writings of C.S. Lewis and others, as he encouraged us to read and think about the stories, which most of us did. Years later, after visiting Oxford University in England, I wondered if this was how C.S. Lewis himself chatted with his students and friends at the famed little restaurant near Madeleine College.

My reverie came to an end as the twelve of us in our close-knit group heard one of the judges call:

"Edinboro High School Girls Ensemble."

I quickly glanced at the eleven girls who were to share this culminating moment in our young lives. Most of them I had known since elementary school. A few were Juniors, the rest of us would graduate the following month. Marilyn, my best friend, for as long as I could remember, and I shared the second alto section.

Marilyn was in love with Mac—deeply in love, as only a high school girl can be with a married man who has become her mentor.

"Marilyn, your feelings for him can't go anywhere," I had cautioned her often.

"I think it will," she replied. "I know he loves me."

"Be careful, kiddo," was all I could think to tell her. "I really, really don't want to see you get hurt."

The stillness of the vaulted ceilings seemed to engulf us all as we made our way quietly to the front of the chapel. None of us had ever sung in such a stunning setting. The other groups that preceded us sounded superb in this acoustically balanced building. We all wondered how we would measure up, yet there had been instilled in us by our dedicated teacher a sense that all our work would be rewarded—that we would represent him and our school and each other well.

We performed two numbers—first the seductive Cole Porter's tune that begins with the words: "You go to my head like a sip of sparkling burgundy brew, and I find the very mention of you like the kicker in a julep or two."

Though only kids, some conception of the intoxicating elements of the piece came through to our minds, perhaps vicariously from our director. Without actually thinking about it, we were aware that he was a man who understood the excitement of cocktails and so much more of the world than any of us had, as yet, experienced.

Under his direction, the song was sung as though we were all twenty years older and wiser. Again, our director's knowledge of these things was instilled in us as if we had experienced much more of life already with this intriguing man. Perhaps, in a way, we each had our own "love affair," of sorts, with him, though none of us knew what an affair even really meant—except perhaps for Marilyn—dear, silly, sophisticated, beautiful, Broadway-aspiring, and vulnerable Marilyn. Marilyn knew.

The first piece was behind us. We knew we had performed it lovingly and well.

We quietly began singing our second and final number: "Softly now the nightingale ...". The complex and haunting piece came forth from our twelve, unified voices. This was the chance we had for our small, college-town school, a hundred miles north of Pittsburgh, to place in the Pennsylvania State music finals.

"If you can't hear the person next to you, you're singing too loud," Mac had told us over and over.

I could hear Marilyn's voice, and I quickly made sure I was not singing louder than she and that my voice was blending with hers and the others in perfect, four-part harmony.

We sang as one. The music was good, and we all knew it was good. Everything we had worked months to accomplish peaked with the final phrases of this song, filling each of us with a great depth of emotion.

Mac, standing apart from us, lowered his head as we finished. That movement of his seemed a benediction; it spoke more than a smile or any words could have conveyed.

Then we waited.

Within a half hour results were posted near the entrance to the chapel doors.

First Place: Edinboro High School Girls Ensemble.

All of us knew joy that day—not just the joy of winning a coveted reward for our work but the joy of having been as one, of blending perfectly, of pleasing a demanding director, as well as the judges, and of taking another step in the remarkable and complicated process of leaving our girlhood behind.

Roger MacDougall, meanwhile, took Marilyn in his stride. He never left his wife and children and later accepted a teaching job at a university in Central Pennsylvania. After several years there, he became terribly disfigured and crippled from a fire that started when he fell asleep smoking a cigarette in bed. A few years later he was killed while attempting to cross a street.

Though talented, Marilyn never made it to Broadway. After earning a teaching degree, she realized immediately that teaching was not for her. Instead, she became an airline stewardess. Then, following what seemed like a loveless marriage, she divorced and left the airline job she loved, a requirement of the airlines for divorcees at that time.

Keeping in touch at least yearly all our adult lives, I watched as my friend led a lonely and frustrated life. Single and without the children she had always hoped she would have, Marilyn moved to Missouri, and in her later years took a demanding and difficult job in an upholstery factory—still pretty, still sophisticated, but admittedly unfulfilled.

After our children were raised, my husband Dean and I, on a cross country trip, looked her up in her little home in the Midwest. Her excitement at seeing us was evident. We chatted and reminisced, and before leaving, Marilyn said, "Do you remember that wonderful day at Heinz Chapel in Pittsburgh?"

She smiled, stroking one of several cats that sat on the couch beside her.

"Oh, yes, of course I do," I replied.

"You know that was the most wonderful day of my entire life."

I understood, shaking my head—showing that I did.

After talking a little more and then taking Marilyn to dinner, Dean and I drove away, waving goodbye as we left her. I knew I was leaving behind a dear friend and also a very special memory—one that the two of us had shared throughout our lives.

A TIME OF MARRIAGE

ME AND MY PENNSYLVANIA DUTCHMAN

"I think it's time," I said quietly, nudging Dean, who was lying beside me, from a sound sleep.

It was after midnight, and I had been experiencing ongoing contractions for several hours.

Married three years, we had hoped to have a baby all that time and were so happy to finally have one coming.

"Are you okay?" Dean asked immediately as he threw the covers aside, rising to grab his pants. "Do we have everything we need?" he asked.

I just smiled.

"We're okay," I replied, "We'll be fine."

And so we were … when five grueling hours later our first baby boy, Glenn David, changed the two of us into a threesome.

And so it was that Dean stood by me, through one of the major transitions of our lives together.

And so he has stood by me, steadfast and unfailing, through all the joys and sorrows of a lifetime—including the births of four more sons, the deaths of our parents and others dear to us, the joys of adding five daughters-in-law to our family, as the years sped by, as well as the births of all of our beautiful grandchildren, the gut-wrenching health problems of two of our sons that necessitated painful, major surgeries, and so much more that life brings to most of us in its inexorable passage.

Dean and I said our "Hellos" to one another the day we met in a high school study hall in the little college town of Edinboro, Pennsylvania. He was the good-looking, new Senior who had just moved into town. He jokingly says that every girl in the school was making a play for him and that I was the lucky one to catch him. (I, on the other hand, think it might just have been the other way around.)

My darling, Dean, had been a good student in his early years of schooling but had "sluffed off" when he began running with some less desirable friends his last couple of years in high school. I, meanwhile, as a high school Junior was a year behind him and had always been a conscientious student—a "teacher's pet," as Dean sometimes called me.

We began dating regularly as soon as we met, both feeling an immediate and strong attraction for each other. We talked of marriage at a young age. However, I had concerns because Dean seemed to have virtually no sense of direction for his life. That summer, following his graduation, he was working on a highway construction job and pumping gas at a service station.

The two of us sat one warm, summer evening on a big, old log lying by the shores of serene Lake Edinboro. In the midst of our musings, I said pointedly to Dean, "Why don't you think about going to college?" and he replied without hesitation, "I hadn't really thought about it, but, you know, I think I will"—and so he did, graduating with a teaching degree four years later.

After my own high school graduation, I spent a semester at the same college, since my parents were still living in Edinboro. Then I decided to move with them to Pittsburgh, 100 miles away, to work at the U.S. Steel Corporation where I began saving money for my forthcoming marriage to Dean.

During these early dating days, my parents had reservations about Dean. Only later did I learn that they hoped my time away from him would persuade me against the marriage, but this was not to be the case. They were concerned about whether he was really committed to an education, and they had major concerns about some of his not-so-great habits at the time, especially those of smoking, drinking, and some of his other "rough edges," as they called them.

Somehow, I seemed to be able to see beyond all of this—or perhaps love really is blind, as the saying goes, for I was surely in love with this boy who was so fascinating to me, so unlike anyone I had known in my young life.

One of our sons, Robb, now jokes that his parents were the reverse of the movie, "Grease," where the girl ultimately goes her wayward boyfriend's direction rather than holding onto her own ideals and standards. Our son says he's been glad that his Dad, on the other hand, chose to go a more positive direction in his life. Robb jokes that he otherwise might not have had his own turn on earth—at least not in what he feels would have been such favorable circumstances.

Dean would come to visit me as often as he could while we lived 100 miles apart, and when a visit had been planned, I could hardly bear the passage of the hours until I saw his car pull up outside my parents' home.

Few people we tell can even imagine the two of us, when we were apart those five years preceding our marriage—which was most of the time—wrote to each other *every single day*—short notes, to be sure, but write daily we did.

To his credit, Dean did quit his too-frequent consumption of beer almost immediately, and shortly after handed me a half-empty pack of cigarettes. He said simply, "That's it." He later told me that quitting smoking, after several years of the habit, was the hardest thing he ever did.

As to Dean's education (and with my parents' urging), we waited to marry until he finished his Bachelor's degree. Our wedding ceremony took place in a little chapel near the University of Pittsburgh, just a week after his graduation. By then my mother and father were more accepting of the marriage than they had been when we first met. By this time they, too, could see Dean's potential, and they also enjoyed his wonderful sense of humor.

Dr. Lou Hendricks, one of Dean's caustic professors at Edinboro, also acknowledged the change. At graduation, he said to Dean, "Hoch, when I first met you, I thought there was one place for you and that was six feet under. I've had to eat my words, and I want to congratulate you for what you've accomplished these past few years."

Dean not only finished his Bachelor's degree, he went on to earn a Master's degree at Cal Poly in San Luis Obispo, California. The two of us had chosen to move there two years after our marriage, and it was there that our first son was born.

A few years later Dean decided to go on to earn a Doctorate in Educational Administration at the University of California at Berkeley. Both of his advanced degrees became a united effort on both our parts, since I typed most of his papers, as well as his 300-page doctoral dissertation. This latter, and lengthy, exercise involved what seemed like endless drafts and revisions—pre-word-processing days. Every time a mistake was made, the page had to be re-typed; every change in a footnote could involve the re-typing of sometimes an entire section. "Argggh," as Charles Schultz often had his comic strip character say.

Where many couples at Berkeley divorced during the doctoral-earning stresses, fortunately our marriage came closer together. I often felt I earned the same degree Dean did. The laugh line at the time for marriages that did hold together was that the wife earned her "Ph.T." (Putting Hubby Through).

With Dean's encouragement, the ink on my own bachelor's and master's degrees would come a little later on, after our little ones were in school. Dean kept his promise to help, as he always did—a superb quality in an individual.

Thinking further about Dean and our life together, I have pondered what makes a person overcome past negative habits and become not only industrious but also faithful, steadfast, and dedicated to worthy purposes and pursuits in life, as well as totally committed to home and family.

Part of the process is making the choice to live by time-tested, bedrock principles that are right and good. I have felt that, perhaps in Dean's case, at least many of these principles and qualities can be credited to those inherited in his genes and DNA—put simply, his ancestry.

He and I have had the fun of pursuing America's #1 hobby of genealogy together. We found both his maternal and paternal lines going back many generations into Germany, Switzerland and Austria.

Through some detailed research, we were able to trace his father's family all the way to his seventh great-grandfather, Rudolph Hoch, who was born in 1683 in the little village of Liestal, near Basel, in Switzerland. The Hoch name, by the way, rhymes with "Coke," and means "high" in German.

Father of two sons, Rudolph Hoch was an Anabaptist, one of those courageous individuals who fought against the powerful Roman Catholic Church in the Middle Ages. The Anabaptists believed that infants were not in need of baptism—only those old enough to understand the meaning of the ordinance. Many of the Anabaptists were, unfortunately, martyred by the powerful, medieval church for their beliefs. Others, like Rudolph and his wife, Veronica, fled the country and emigrated to a land free from the intolerable religious persecution of the day.

For Rudolph, this place was in the New World, in the rolling hills of Eastern Pennsylvania. Others of Dean's ancestors—with names such as Shaffer, Brocious, Haas, Hinderliter, and Mattern, (the family for whom the Matterhorn Mountain in Switzerland was named)—also emigrated from various parts of Germany, Switzerland, and Austria. Settling in the green countryside northwest of Philadelphia, they collectively became known—and are known to this day—as the Pennsylvania Dutch (or Deutsche).

Many later ventured over the Allegheny Mountains in the early 1800's and settled in Western Pennsylvania where Dean was born generations later near the historic, little town of Punxsutawney—of groundhog weather-predicting fame. All of those early settlers could be considered pioneers of the finest sort—adventuresome, hard-working, dedicated to religious ideals, independent, stoic, yet with a life-easing sense of humor.

A goodly number of Dean's Hoch ancestors were Mennonites, similar to the Amish, but more liberal in their views. They were extremely hardworking, industrious people who built for themselves a new way of life on America's early frontier.

After their long voyage from Switzerland in 1717—decades before the American Revolution—Rudolph, Veronica, and their two sons, Johannes and Melchior, made their way northwest from Philadelphia, settling on a plot of acreage in the lush, green Oley Valley near Reading. They built a large, beautiful flagstone farmhouse still in use—and still in the Hoch name—after almost three centuries. The farm has a look, as well as a setting, and also a barn, much like that in the Harrison Ford movie "Witness." The farm has been placed on the Register of National Historic Sites.

Rudolph and Veronica are buried in the fenced, gated cemetery plot on the farm, along with other family members who later fought to unyoke America from the tyranny of England during the Revolutionary War. Others of the family, including Dean's great-grandfather, David William Hoch, fought decades later in the Civil War's Union Army—this time to unyoke our nation's blacks from the unconscionable institution of slavery.

What a proud and steadfast heritage for this strong, resolute man I married.

As I often look at Dean in quiet moments, pondering all the goodness that is part of him, I feel a reassuring sense of gratitude for his always being there—for putting me and our children ahead of so many attractive enticements and selfish attitudes that pull so many marriages apart.

It's been said that it's not a bad idea to write one's own epitaph. With a smile, Dean quickly dashed off what he would like to have written on his own gravestone:

"A GOOD HUSBAND, A GOOD FATHER AND GRANDFATHER, AND HE MADE PEOPLE LAUGH."

As far as I am concerned, he has fully lived that epitaph.

Besides which, in all our years together, I maintain that there's never been a dull moment. That has to be a tribute to Dean as well. People often tell us that the two of us have lived three lifetimes in one, and I believe that is true.

As to his being a good husband, I have always liked simply being with him. He has been my companion, my lover, my friend. We have laughed together and cried together. Though so very different in our outlooks and personalities, we nevertheless have complimented each other and brought out the best in each other throughout our lives. Neither of us would have accomplished all we have in life without the synergy we have created. We have also done our best to make each other's dreams come true.

Just one example of his caring began on a winter evening, when he and I were out shopping. I took a terrific fall on a patch of ice and suffered a skull fracture and serious brain injury.

The attending neurosurgeon told Dean that, "With a fall such as this, one of two things usually happens: The person is either dead or a vegetable."

Dr. Robert Atkins, the diet guru, took a fall similar to mine just a few weeks later in New York City, and he died within a few weeks.

During the month that followed my fall, I experienced severe headaches and double vision, followed by a total loss of my ability to ever smell again. Dean took wonderful care of me until I recovered, and I couldn't have asked for a kinder, more diligent nurse.

As to being a good father, he taught our five sons to work hard, to be honest in their dealings, and to give to their mother their highest level of respect. He played with them, took them on trips, and taught them what commitment to home and family is all about. He has always cared about each one of them so very much, and he loves each of them beyond measure. Even as married men, they still call him and ask for his advice and counsel, and he places an extremely high value on his continuing association with each of them.

As to his making people laugh, I have watched him do that every chance he gets—watching for any opportunity to lighten a conversation or a tense situation. He sees the absurd side of just about everything and turns it into a quip or a joke. It is fun to be with him. He sincerely believes, as a sage old gentleman once said, "If you can't see the humor around you, you're missing half your life."

Does he have faults? Of course.

Probably, also from his heritage, he can put on his demanding and bossy hat at times and often wants me to "Hurry up." He likes using the old British expression, "Let's get cracking,"—often when my slower nature resists being rushed about. On the other hand, he does not always follow through on certain activities, himself, as quickly as I think he should.

He manages to forever be sorting his papers and newspapers all over the office and living room floors. He leaves his clothes in piles on our cedar chest instead of putting them in the closet, and he drips water all over the kitchen and bathroom sinks and doesn't wipe it up. Small matters? Of course—nevertheless sources of irritation to me at times.

However, I am all too well aware that he tolerates what he calls my "obsessive-compulsive, Type A personality," and I, on the other hand, have learned to tolerate those things about him that drive me "round the bend" (a British expression from my own heritage).

"Hey," I say to myself, "look at all the good things about him." And I know he says the same thing to himself about me and my quirks.

And so it has been throughout the decades of our marriage. The two of us have wandered the road of life, grateful for the ride—over the bumps, down into the deep valleys and upward, time and again, to experience the wonderful vistas from those exhilarating and breath-taking mountain tops.

It has not always been an easy go, but gratefully we have done it all—and we have done it together ... me and my Pennsylvania Dutchman.

"UNTO ONE OF THE LEAST OF THESE"

"Hi … Wow! How come the house is such a mess?" my husband asked nonchalantly as he came through the door.

It was not at all what I wanted to hear.

"If you think it's such a mess, you can clean it up yourself," I snapped back at him.

As is sometimes, but rarely the case, the man I married did not seem to understand that it had been one of *those* days: hurried, hectic, and harried. It was obvious to me, as well as to him, that it was one of those rare days when the dishes were still in the sink, the bed not made, and piles of paper stacked everywhere for sorting and filing.

The problem certainly wasn't lack of desire to have things neat and tidy. The Biblical "Mary/Martha principle" had been in place, with a hospital visit to a sick neighbor and some important child care needs taking precedence over the other tasks of the day. In that regard, I felt I had "chosen the better part," but it didn't help the fact that I had come home tired from my visits and other essential errands.

I was certainly not prepared for a husband who, if I had stopped to think about it, had also had a difficult and challenging day. Though we'd been married for many years and had now and then gone through these sorts of days before, this time was different.

Dean had often said that our disagreements were usually over the silliest of things—things just like this incident—and he was right.

It seems the Adversary takes every opportunity to put wedges between husbands and wives, and it's something every couple needs to recognize and guard against. However, as we all know, that's not always easy to do.

This particular day, after my sharp retort was already spoken, a scripture came with great force to my mind and heart: ***"Inasmuch as ye have done it unto one of the least of these my brethren, ye have done it unto me."***

The thought that followed was that my husband was far from "one of the least of these." He was and is my dearest companion and friend.

Would I speak this way to the Savior? Would any of us be sharp, sarcastic, or unkind in addressing the Redeemer of the World? Obviously not. Then why are we so prone to do this with those we love the most?

Since that day, and because that scripture came so forcefully to my mind, I've been much more careful about the way I speak to my sweetheart.

I do my best to curb my tongue and sometimes write a quick note to express my feelings rather than getting into a verbal sparring match.

When I think of the words I speak as being directed to the Lord, it causes me to be so much more careful. I've observed that when I put this principle fully into practice, the spirit is catching. My husband seems to be much kinder in the way *he* speaks. Our home is a happier place because we are both reflecting the Gospel (or Good News) more fully within its walls.

BEING MARRIED AT MIDLIFE AIN'T BAD EITHER

An article appeared in our local paper, the *Idaho State Journal*, written by a regular contributor, Penelope Reedy, under her slogan "My Private Pocatello." An instructor at Idaho State University, she had titled this particular feature: "Being single at midlife isn't necessarily a bad thing." The piece extolled what she felt were the advantages of being single in her late Fifties and included the idea of not having to "daily accommodate another person's idiosyncrasies," and later in the piece "not having to fix a real breakfast or listen to a man gargle and hack up phlegm every morning." She also added that, following her divorce and now in midlife, she is free to think as she pleases.

Reading the column, I felt impelled to write a response article which was published a few weeks later. I wanted to speak for those of us who take the opposite view—that there is a special joy of being happily married at midlife—the reward, if you will, for having spent a lifetime accommodating another person's idiosyncrasies, as my own marriage partner has accommodated my idiosyncrasies for so many years (and I his, of course). The two of us think we've learned, in decades of commitment to marriage, at least a little of what the institution is all about.

Ms. Reedy's column also stated that "For all life's disruptions and the sadness about 'what might have been' that divorce causes, the freedom from emotional bondage far outweighs other difficulties …"

I wholeheartedly agree with the first part of this statement but vehemently decry the unnecessary divorces that are causing the disintegration of families across our nation. Obviously, there are a small number of marriages that must, unfortunately, end in divorce, but far too many couples allow selfishness and unadulterated self-interest tear apart that which was joined by vitally important covenants and promises.

Be that as it may, I for one, am grateful to have been blessed with a good marriage—one that my husband and I both have worked hard to make a success—and, believe me, we've had our share of ups and downs.

This idea of building a marriage, of course, is never an easy effort, especially when both partners have strong personalities and varying political and social opinions. (Note: Thinking for myself led to the two of us canceling each other's votes for a goodly number of years—until he "saw the light"—and we still get into some lively and heated discussions about the world and its problems.) It's my sincere belief that those sharp differences in our marriage are what have made our union both exciting and dynamic over the years.

Together we raised our family of five sons—with my husband always putting our family ahead of his other interests. We have watched those sons grow and marry five caring and lovely young women who are all bright and perceptive and who have chosen to be (and are able to be) stay-at-home moms while their children are small. Thankfully, they and their husbands are committed to making their own marriages and families work, in spite of all the inherent challenges in the world today. We constantly pray for their success in this most important of all occupations. What else, after all, impacts the world for generations to come as does a successful (or unsuccessful) family?

Meanwhile, my husband and I feel a certain satisfaction as we near the "end of the road," knowing that we've been able to hold it together. We have the fun of now enjoying things we couldn't do when the kids were all at home. We share a sweet and special closeness as we realize our time together grows shorter with each passing day.

It's just simply nice at this time of life to have a marriage partner to walk with, talk with, to think about and care for. Even as a young girl, I loved seeing older couples walking hand in hand, witnessing their devotion to one another to the end of their days.

Now I find the two of us are one of those older couples.

I once heard this sage advice from a respected authority on marriage:

"The fact is that most putts don't drop. Most beef is tough.... Most successful marriages require a high degree of mutual toleration. Most jobs are more often dull than otherwise....

"Life is like an old-time rail journey—delays, sidetracks, smoke, dust, cinders, and jolts, interspersed only occasionally by beautiful vistas and thrilling bursts of speed....

"The trick is to thank the Lord for letting you have the ride."

Yes, I'm convinced that being married at midlife is just a part of that "old-time rail journey," a special and wonderful blessing—one I wish every couple could enjoy.

A TIME OF FAMILY

OUR FRUIT OF THE LOOMS/
LAKE TAHOE ADVENTURE

Fall introduces itself subtly to the foothills of the Sierra Nevada Mountains. The air cools gradually, and tinges of color in the leaves announce the inevitability of winter approaching. It was an October day in this changing season when we decided to take our brood of boys for a weekend at Lake Tahoe.

An advantage of living in the Sacramento area is its close proximity to many exciting places … just an hour and a half to San Francisco, three or four hours to Yosemite, the same to the historic Napa Valley wine country, and even less to Tahoe and the Nevada border.

Two or three times a year we headed in the latter direction to Lake Tahoe, sometimes to enjoy the deep, clear waters of Tahoe's alpine lake, sometimes to explore Reno and the nearby restored ghost town of Virginia City, and sometimes just to take in dinner and a stage show at one of the casinos.

On our occasional excursions to the city of Lake Tahoe in the mid-Seventies, all the boys looked forward to a couple of hours in the supervised kid's center while the two of us enjoyed dinner and the entertainment of some big name stars.

For this particular trip we decided to give the boys a little more freedom and independence than usual in packing, prompted by the fact that it was a last-minute decision to go, and we were in a hurry to get on the road. We said to them, "Okay, guys, this time everybody packs their own duds. It's only an over-nighter, so put what you need in your backpacks, and let's get on our way.

Glenn, at age 16, was no problem, and we had confidence that even our youngest, Greg, nearing age seven, we thought could manage a change of clothes and a toothbrush. So, within the hour we all piled into our Volkswagen van, which we called "somewhat psychedelic," because it was factory-adorned with bright, vivid colors of chartreuse, yellow, and blue.

Off we went on Route 50 headed northeast.

On the way, we stopped for gas at Placerville. Near this quiet little community, gold was discovered in the mid 1800s, and the world was forever changed.

Placerville, however, almost as its name sounds, settled down after the boom and still remained placid and peaceful in its Sierra Nevada foothills setting.

Pulling into the station, we spotted a young man of about 25 dressed in a clean white T-shirt and an equally clean pair of white slacks. With blond hair and blue eyes, he presented a neat impression. On his back was a tidy bedroll and backpack, and in his hands a hitchhiker's sign that read simply "Berlin." Having a German name like "Hoch," we were intrigued, so we engaged him in conversation.

"Are you actually heading for Germany?" was our first query.

His accent left no doubt. He might as well have said, "Jawohl."

The boys were all quiet and seemed fascinated with the stranger and particularly his manner of speech.

"Yes," he replied politely," "I am hitchhiking from San Francisco to New York, and from there I will decide how to go the rest of the way. Do you happen to be heading toward Nevada?"

Though we made it a policy never to pick up hitchhikers, it just seemed natural to say, "Sure. Would you like a ride as far as Lake Tahoe?"

He was appreciative of the offer, and the boys quickly made room for him in the van. We joked about the vehicle being of German make. Within minutes, the eight of us were wending our way through the winding roads and high pines of the Sierra foothills. The conversation that ensued was memorable.

"Ever been to America before?" we asked.

"No," was the reply.

"What brings you to this part of the U.S.?" We asked.

"Well," he said slowly in broken English, "I've spent the past two months in Japan teaching English to the Japanese. I had planned to stay two years, but I'm afraid I developed a bad case of culture shock almost as soon as I arrived. The Japanese with their black hair and dark eyes all began to look alike to me, and I felt terribly out of place. So I'm having to give up the whole idea and head back home."

"Are you really thinking of hitchhiking all the way across the U.S. at this time of year?"

"Yes," he said simply.

All we could envision was his seemingly woeful lack of warm clothing and supplies and what we gathered was a total lack of understanding as to just how big America is. We felt it was not our place, however, to intervene in his plans.

Entering the city of Lake Tahoe, we came to the California/Nevada border, and our guest was amazed that there were no guards, nor even a requirement to stop. This of course, was in the days prior to the fall of the Berlin Wall.

"What, no checkpoint?" he asked.

We laughed and said at that time there were no restrictions, except agricultural checks, between any of the States and very few even between Canada and the U.S. or Mexico and the U.S. He exhibited amazement.

Equally amazed, he shook his head when we told him we had driven two hours just to see a show and that we planned to drive home again early in the morning. We could see that in Germany this kind of trip would have been highly unlikely for him. He seemed the type who preferred much more planning, much less spontaneity, and not so hurried an overnighter.

Arriving at the casino, we invited our new friend to be our guest for the show. He declined our offer, however, so we let him out of the van, and he was off on his way to find another ride. Waving goodbye, we wished him well.

Our brief encounter reminded us how much alike we citizens of the earth really are—and yet how different we often allow ourselves to be in our attitudes of race, religion, customs, and nationalities. We had felt an immediate rapport with our European friend, but he had not been able to bridge the Oriental/Occidental gap. That same adventure was yet to be experienced by us years later when we visited Japan and China ourselves.

Obviously, for a multiplicity of reasons, some people are comfortable with all kinds of differences in their relationships. For others, these same differences seem to present an insurmountable challenge.

Meanwhile, we enjoyed the show immensely. The boys had a great time and later, in our motel, we all had a big laugh when our "littlest," Greg, unpacked his bag. There was no change of clothes, no pajamas, and no toothbrush. All this dear, young lad had felt necessary to pack for his overnighter were eight pairs of Size 6 "Fruit of the Loom" underwear.

THE INTRUDER

The intruder forced its way into our home—unbidden, unwanted, and hurtful—interrupting the normal ebb and flow of our everyday lives. Had we had the power, we would have done everything to prevent it from becoming a part of us.

However, the choice was not ours, and we simply had to deal with a force that suddenly was a part of us and would be for many years to come.

It happened when our son, Barry, was just six years old.

Shortly before his seventh birthday on December 17, my husband and I, along with Barry and his four brothers, were all off in our Volkswagen van. We were heading for a day in the Northern California foothills. It was typical for us to do this when a sunny afternoon presented itself—and we had the urge to play rather than work. We would quickly pack some peanut butter and jelly sandwiches, carrot sticks, cookies and drinks, and off we would go.

This particular day, as we traveled, Barry asked several times to stop so that he could go to the bathroom. Driver Dad was patient, to a point, but finally he growled gently at his first grader and said, "Hey, Barry, maybe if you didn't drink so much, you wouldn't have to stop at every service station on the way."

Barry gave us his puppy-dog, somewhat quizzical look. He lifted his little shoulders as if to say, "Gee, I'm sorry; I can't help it."

The problem continued, however, and we noticed the same scenario again on another short trip we took within the next week.

At home, Barry seemed sluggish and not quite his peppy self. However, he perked up as his birthday approached, and we had our usual celebration with hats made from newspapers, cake and ice cream, and five special friends.

Then Christmas was upon us.

A few weeks later, on January 15, my mother died and our oldest son, Glenn, and I flew back for a weekend to attend her funeral in Pennsylvania. It was not an easy time.

Immediately upon my return, I noticed a definite change in Barry, and I regretted not having taken him to the doctor sooner. However, with five boys, Dean and I had learned not to dash off too quickly to the Kaiser medical facility located a half-hour from our home. Over the years, we had found that most of our kids' minor health problems resolved themselves, and we had also learned to trust in nature's wonderful cures for common ailments. The change in our son was apparent enough, however, that I made an appointment immediately.

On that rainy afternoon, Barry and I got out of the car in the huge, downtown Sacramento medical center parking lot and headed for our one o'clock meeting with Dr. Coop, our pediatrician. I took Barry's small hand in mine and said to him, "Hurry, honey; we'll be late."

He looked up at me, and said simply, "I can't hurry, Mommy; I'm just too tired."

This wasn't like our thin and lively little boy, and his inability to hurry caused me added alarm.

Our punctual, young doctor, whom we had known for years, saw us immediately. He lifted Barry onto the examining table, and I explained the somewhat vague symptoms our son had been experiencing. He felt Barry's glands, listened to his heart and lungs, then placed a tongue depressor in his mouth and smelled his breath. An immediate urine test brought the dreaded words, "Nancy, we'll have to put your little fellow in the hospital right away. He has diabetes."

A slap across the face could not have hit me harder. Neither Dean nor I had any idea of the symptoms of this disease: frequent urination, excessive thirst, and general fatigue, symptoms that Barry had been exhibiting. Had we known, of course, we would have had Barry to the doctor much sooner. As it was, we thought he had a flu bug that had gone through everyone else in the family with the same general symptoms Barry had. Our ignorance allowed the disease to progress to the point where Barry's blood sugar level was dangerously high.

Dr. Coop did not chastise me. He and I simply walked from his office, along with Barry, to the hospital section of the facility where Barry was admitted.

The admission procedures were like a wildly disturbing dream. Insulin was administered at once, and Barry was given a gown and placed in a pediatric bed. All the charts, and tests, and seeing the various technicians working with him only accentuated the seriousness of his condition to my reeling mind.

I quickly learned that Barry had childhood onset or Type I diabetes. The cause remains unknown, and there is no cure.

When Barry was settled in his hospital bed, I walked to the hallway and phoned Dean at the elementary school where he was serving as principal. I asked his secretary to put me through as quickly as possible. When he came on the line, I said, through a voice choked with tears, "Our little boy has a big problem, honey. He has diabetes."

For a time Dean said nothing. Both of us had known diabetics, and we knew the disease was serious. We understood immediately that a lifetime of care would be needed.

Obviously, no parents want illness to enter their child's life, especially chronic illness—a challenge we had never had to face. However, without question, we knew we could lean on each other—and that we would both support and help our son. I knew Dean would stand by me, and I by him, and both of us by Barry, whatever the future might hold. Somehow we felt that unspoken assurance to be a special strength.

"I'll be there right away," Dean said, and I knew he would hurry to be with us.

From that eventful day, the regimen of life with diabetes has affected all our lives. We have learned and grown from what we have experienced—Barry, his brothers, our extended family, and, of course, Dean and myself.

Following the days in the hospital and our return home, the latent period set in when Barry's need for insulin dropped dramatically. We had been told by the doctor that it would appear Barry was getting well and would no longer need insulin but that this was simply a phenomenon of the disease.

We were also told, however, not to allow ourselves any false hopes. It was hard not to, but the doctors were right. The disease finally stabilized, and we began the daily routine of living with the severest form of diabetes.

Learning to give the shots was an exacting process and terribly difficult for me to do.

"I don't think I can push those needles into his little body," I told my dear Dean outside earshot of our son. However, both of us had to learn to do just that, practicing first on an orange, then gritting our teeth as we injected the daily needles with the life-giving substance into the soft, thin, flesh of our son's upper arms, thighs, and buttocks.

We rotated the injections so damage would not be done to the tissues because of repetition to the same spot. As he became a little older, Barry took on this task of giving his injections himself—a task not easy for him either.

I hated seeing him have to deal with this. He, however, simply made the best of what had to be, and his father and I had to do the same. I admired the strength of one so young.

Then came the urine tests and later, as the years went on, the more accurate pricking of his finger several times a day to test his blood. Mixing of various kinds of insulin and multiple shots of the substance each day helped in the striving for more normal blood sugar levels that were necessary to prevent complications.

Only ten percent of the nation's millions of diabetics are of the Type I, insulin-dependent and usually childhood-onset variety. The disease for these people is more serious than for their adult-onset counterparts. The pancreas simply quits functioning. Some theories suggest a viral infection and others an inherited factor as the cause. Whatever the reason, the disease is doubly difficult as youngsters grow and develop, particularly as they go through adolescence with its many bodily changes.

Barry, however, a tough and gutsy kid, tried hard not to let his disease hold him back. He did well in school, went on his Scout outings, and even participated in a 50-mile troop hike in the Sierra Nevada Mountains—a hike his father accompanied him on that measured closer to seventy miles rather than the originally planned fifty.

His brothers were there for him as he grew—two older and two younger. When an occasional hypoglycemic reaction occurred, caused by too much insulin, Barry would get groggy. We all knew to get orange juice or some sugar into his system. Occasionally the reaction would cause him to lose consciousness, and sometimes a shot of glucagon had to be administered to bring him around.

Over time, all of us learned to deal with the stresses and strains—the ups and downs of diabetes, and we became a stronger family. We became educated in dealing with adversity, and we believed there was a purpose in all we were experiencing.

Barry, of course, faced the biggest challenge, and he faced it well. Now an adult, he has come to know and understand what Rose Kennedy, matriarch of the Kennedy clan, once said: "I hope my grandchildren and great-grandchildren will have courage and strength to bear the inevitable difficulties and disappointments and griefs of life—bear them with dignity and without self-pity. Knowing that tragedies befall everyone, and that although one may seem singled out for special sorrows, that is not really so; that worse things have happened many times to others in the world, and that it is not tears, but determination that makes pain bearable."

Of all the major diseases, diabetes perhaps stands one of the greatest chances of being cured. The future of the ongoing research looks promising, and many strides have been made toward this end. We pray every day for that dreamed of breakthrough to come—and, with parents everywhere whose children have this disease, we pray that it will come soon.

Although neither Barry nor any of the rest of us can say the intrusion of diabetes has become welcome to us, we can say that we adjusted ourselves to this unwanted development in our lives. We tried harder each day to understand, to accommodate, to communicate, and to not feel rejection but acceptance of what this intruder, or may we say "teacher," has brought to us.

A scripture from the Bible says, "In all things, give thanks." This is not easy to do.

How do we give thanks when harsh adversity enters our lives?

In our family's situation, pondering this, we came to understand that we can:

Give thanks this was something we could learn to live with.

Give thanks that what we had to deal with was not any worse.

Give thanks we could learn and grow and empathize with others who have similar problems.

Give thanks for Barry's strength and fortitude.

Give thanks for his great laugh and that he could continue to be a part of our lives and not taken from us.

Give thanks that Dean and I could somehow grow closer by sharing all that is required when a child faces a major challenge, knowing this is often not the case.

Give thanks for the opportunity we have to try to set good examples for our children and grandchildren, as they come to face their own Gethsemanes.

Give thanks for the knowledge that the Savior took upon himself sorrow we will never comprehend and that He knows and understands all our pain.

Give thanks, also, for the knowledge that our cares and sorrows, though hard to endure, are temporary—that our mortal lives are only a dot on the line of our eternal journey.

Yes, there is great room for giving thanks, and truly, tho' life is hard, yet "with blessings unmeasured, our cup runneth o'er."

THE GENERAL STORE

Embarking on one's own business has been part of the American way of life since the days of Benjamin Franklin and the Colonials. Embarking on a family business can be even more exciting, especially when children are quite small. The possibilities are endless, if parents look for them, and the learning experience is something that cannot be achieved in any other way.

Children who are part of even a limited family business can be taught the principles of hard work, creativity, ingenuity, as well as the practical applications of skills such as accounting, advertising, sales, communication, and product development, not to mention the values of honesty and integrity in a commercial setting.

Even the simplest of home businesses can bring much of this kind of learning. At our Fair Oaks, California home, an idea we tried was selling some rather unusual kitchen items out of our home. We met a young man who was making small wheat grinders in his garage. We were into healthy eating, liked to bake our own homemade bread, and enjoyed having freshly ground whole wheat flour to make the bread even more healthy and delicious.

We combined the wheat grinders with a sleek bread mixing machine from England, the Kenwood, which we were able to buy wholesale, and we found ourselves in a home business which became highly successful.

None of us in the family considered ourselves to be entrepreneurs. I had even been intimidated, as a child, selling Girl Scout cookies; in fact, I hated it. However, this set of kitchen items that we began to share with our friends was of such excellent value and at such a well-discounted price that I felt we were simply making a wonderful deal available to them. Showing people how to use the machines made the sales not seem like selling at all but more like fun. The effort was taxing at times, but the business began to build quickly, and we were amazed at our success.

Dean, of course, had been trained in education and was working in that field but got involved also, as did the boys. The whole endeavor worked well, actually remarkably well, and we saved enough money in a couple of years to consider buying a little store.

While out for a leisurely drive one day, Dean and I spotted the perfect place … a rather dilapidated brown shingle building in the heart of "Old Towne Fair Oaks," an artsy and quaint community that we felt would lend itself beautifully to an old-fashioned general store concept.

As the whole idea took shape, I often thought what adventures just about any of us can have in life, if we allow our imaginations full rein. Shakespeare once said, "Our doubts are traitors and make us lose the good we oft might win by fearing to attempt." It was a saying my father had ingrained in me simply by saying it time and again. Such adages can be well worth repeating to our children. Thus we fill their minds—and our own—with positive images that can see us through difficulties and make us better and braver people than we otherwise might be.

Not doubting (at least not too much), we called the real estate agent about the building, assessed all its problems, deducted the costs that we calculated would be needed for renovation from the asking price, and made our offer. To our surprise and delight, the offer was accepted, and it was ours.

There we were—not professional business people in any sense of the word—opening a store. We hardly knew the difference between an accounts receivable and an accounts payable, nor did we have an understanding of most of the other common business terms.

Nevertheless, Dean quit his job as a principal mid-year and, looking back, we realize this was a bold move indeed. However, it made the adrenalin run and the endorphins race. For both of us, failure never entered our minds. The venture was fun and exciting and, best of all, it involved our whole family.

We worked like dogs, as the old saying goes, cleaning and scraping and decorating. Friends helped us hang antiques throughout and place hand-made pink gingham curtains at the windows. Before long we had a store that purposely looked like it had been there a hundred years or more. We called it Doc Hoch's General Store (a take-off from Dean's doctoral degree in education). We geared the establishment mainly toward health foods.

For our grand opening, we hired a bluegrass band to play on the front porch of the building; we arranged horse-drawn hay rides for the kids; I wore a long, Gunny Sac dress, and Dean and the boys wore store-keeper aprons. We quickly built a clientele that included every kind and type of customer from hippies to more conservative types, including the Mayor of the town, Bill Withrow. Bill and his wife, Kathy, came into the store almost daily and became, through this association, our fast friends.

We sold our basic kitchen items, added all kinds and types of foods, grains, and herbs, and even started up a lunch counter where we served soups and sandwiches and the most delicious nutburgers anyone could ever imagine. Following McDonald's lead, Dean creatively put up a sign outside the building that read: "Nutburgers—100 sold," then "150, 325, 949," and so on. People loved it. We never did catch up with the "Big Mac Boys," but we had a great time imitating them, to the delight of our customers.

Dean had a knack for eliciting some great free advertising for the store. For example, when Jimmy Carter was running for President, Dean came up with the idea of calling the president-to-be's brother, Billy Carter, at the family peanut farm in Plains, Georgia.

Billy actually answered the phone, and Dean said, "I'd like to order some raw peanuts in the shell."

Billy replied, in his Southern accent, "How many carloads you 'wont'?"

Dean said, "Not carloads. Just a couple hundred pound sacks will be fine."

When the nuts arrived, we had Lynn, our young secretary, draw a caricature of Jimmy Carter that we duplicated on slips of paper. The message read: "Natural Carter peanuts from Plains, Georgia." We inserted a small quantity of peanuts with the slips of paper in small baggies and gave them away to customers as they checked out.

To our amazement, all four major Sacramento TV stations got wind of what we were doing and sent reporters out from the city to film the nuts being handed out. The intriguing, little news story was picked up by the wire service and aired nationwide.

Dean's mother, 2,500 miles away, sitting on her rocking chair in Pennsylvania, nearly had a heart attack watching the late news and seeing a clip of her son standing in front of the store in his shopkeeper apron. She heard the newscaster say: "An enterprising young entrepreneur in Fair Oaks, California is capitalizing on the upcoming Presidential election to bring customers into his old-fashioned general store…." and so forth—and bring in the customers it did.

Then, the same year at Christmas time, Dean called the Sacramento TV stations himself this time and said, "Would your viewers like to know what frankincense and myrrh look like? We have a supply in our herb jars here in our store in Fair Oaks."

Again, we were amazed that all the major stations responded immediately. They did a captivating holiday story showing these herbs that we had for sale by the ounce.

This kind of free advertising made our store an instant success throughout the greater Sacramento area.

Our boys, meanwhile, worked in the store after school, and all earned a weekly paycheck based mainly on their ages. Early Saturday morning they all helped with the major weekly cleanup. One morning a lady coming into the store just as we were opening and saw all five boys finishing their chores. She said, "This is something wonderful—a family working together. I haven't seen this since I was a young girl back in Vermont. Kids used to have this experience; it was commonplace, but most don't anymore. It's great to see it can still happen." She actually had tears in her eyes.

Even after the store was sold, we did our best to involve our kids in work of one kind or another. It's gratifying now to see that, because of this kind of training, they know how to do a job and do it well—three of them in business, one in drafting, and one in education.

Greg, the youngest, often says, "I used to hate harvesting all those almonds on our acreage in the hot Sacramento summers. All of us guys used to think of every excuse to go inside for a drink or whatever, but Dad would 'crack the whip' and say, 'I'll get a jug of water for everyone. You guys just keep on working,' or 'Mom will be bringing out some sandwiches soon. Just get cracking till the job's done'."

Greg credits those days with giving him and his brothers the knowledge of what hard work is all about. He and his brothers now admit those experiences, while they were growing up, gave them a keen understanding of the truism: "A job well done is time well spent," another adage we felt worth repeating.

Not only that, but the boys were quick to learn the practicalities and the terminologies of business.

For example, shortly after we sold our store to the wife of the producer of the movie, STAR WARS, for a goodly price that was beyond our wildest dreams, we took all the boys to Marriott's Great America amusement park south of San Francisco.

At the gate, we looked at the prices and noted that the entrance fees for seven of us were going to be significant.

Matthew, who was ten at the time said, "Wow! I wonder what they gross here in a day?"

And Robbie, who was seven, popped up and said, "Gross? I wonder what they net?"

Mom and Dad just looked at each other and smiled.

THE SIDEWALK PAINTING CAPER

What's more fun than a eight-year-old boy? Not much, until he and a pal take it into their heads to plaster oil-based paint on an unsuspecting neighbor's sidewalk ... and porch ... and front door.

By and large, our five sons were fearful of getting into any kind of trouble. They had a healthy respect—particularly for their dad's authority—and usually did their utmost not to raise his ire. In short, most of the time they toed the line.

However, as the old maxim goes, "Boys will be boys," and we heard another thought we liked even better. A speaker talking to a large audience on the subject of child-rearing said that, "If parents tell you they never had trouble with their kids, it might lead you to believe they might lie about other things as well."

In a rush to not be placed in the bailiwick with liars, we are willing to admit our boys were not always angels—pretty close—but with skewed halos now and again.

Such was the case with our cute, little eight-year-old, Barry, and his red-haired, freckle-faced sidekick, David Cotton. David lived up the street from our home, and he and Barry became fast friends the day they first met in kindergarten.

David's mother, Margaret, was a highly intelligent woman who had been widowed at age forty. With a congenital hip deformity, she was left with four children to raise, David being the youngest. Our family and theirs shared many good times together—both before and after Harold's death.

David would often come to spend the night at our home, and Barry at David's. David, a demure, quiet little fellow, nevertheless had a Tom Sawyer personality.

One summer afternoon the call came from the Cotton home. It was David. "Can Barry come and spend the night at my house?"

Always insisting on the "double permission" rule, I told David we would check with Barry's Dad as soon as he got home from work to see if he agreed. Then I told him Barry would call back to let him know for sure.

Incidentally, the "double permission rule" saved us much grief and disagreement raising our boys. It was something we learned from a set of parents who had sailed the seas of parenting ahead of us. They simply made it a not-to-be-forgotten rule that any activity of any import had to have the permission of not just Mom, and not just Dad, but *both* parents. If a disagreement arose, it was discussed without the child present.

It's amazing how much frustration and mis-communication this rule saved us over the years. In a two-parent household, kids sometimes tend to "work" the softer parent and go to that individual for the "go-ahead" on an activity. This can lead to difficulty when the other parent has a reason for saying, "No." At any rate, the double permission rule worked well for us and is one we highly recommend.

Dad, as it turned out, had no objection to Barry going to David's for the night. The boys were a compatible pair and never gave us any cause for concern. This night however, proved to be one that now brings smiles, but at the time was quite a shocker.

About ll p.m. the phone rang, and we heard Margaret Cotton's voice.

"You're not going to believe this," she said.

"What is it?" I asked, my curiosity immediately piqued.

"A policeman is here at the house. Our boys have perpetrated something akin to a crime, I'm afraid."

"What?" I said, stunned.

I could tell from her voice that this was not a major crime, but it was still a shock to hear her mention that a policeman was involved.

"We'll be right there," I told her, and Dean and I hurried to her home.

"What on earth did these tykes do?" Dean asked.

The policeman tried to appear stern, but the contrite and repentant looks on our two imps were enough to make anyone smile. However, we did our best to also remain austere. The boys were obviously scared to death.

"We had a call from a neighbor down the street," the officer said. "It appears these two boys decided to decorate her place with a can of orange paint. They did quite a number on her door, her porch, and the sidewalk, too, it seems."

All we could do was express amazement, scowl, and raise our eyebrows at the two young perpetrators.

Talking it over, the adults agreed nothing much could be done until morning, so we hauled our own remorseful youngster home and told him we would be setting things straight on the morrow.

Dean was off to work the next day, so I gave Margaret a call.

"Well, dear friend, what do you think is the best way to teach these two boys of ours a lesson?" I asked.

The two of us thought things through together and decided our best course of action was to put the good old work ethic into play. We decided to have our boys simply clean up the mess they had made.

It didn't matter to either of us which of our sons had been the instigator. Together they had settled on this little prank to play and both, we decided, were to share equally in the restitution.

We later learned that there had been bad blood at school between the boy who lived in the house and our two, and that this rancor had precipitated the incident. We like to think that neither Barry nor David knew that their "enemy's" mother, was a widow woman with a badly crippled arm. When this came to everyone's knowledge, it seemed all the more important that her property be restored to its original state, if at all possible.

It turned out the project would be as much work for the two moms as it was for the boys. Early the next day the four of us took cloths, wire scrapers, paint remover, and other items to the site and began the laborious process of removing all the oil base paint. The boys did the lion cubs' share of the work, but being so young they were not able to fully take on the entire cleanup task themselves. However, to their credit, they worked hard. Uncomplainingly, they spent the day by our sides until the entire job was done.

I really cannot say how David and Barry, as adults now themselves, think back on this event in their lives. Both are married and have children of their own. However, I know the day is not forgotten. Barry still mentions it now and again with a wry smile.

For me, looking back, the experience was *almost* fun. Even then, it was almost fun.

During the day we spent together, Margaret and I chuckled from time to time as we visited and worked side by side. We talked lightly about the lesson we were trying to teach our sons. Neither of us wanted to preach to them or berate them. We simply wanted them to learn from a mistake—something every human being needs to do.

The four of us just pitched in and did our best to set something that was wrong right again—and there is almost always a goodly measure of satisfaction in that kind of activity.

THE PUGILISTIC PEACE PRIZE KID

Most parents teach their kids that fighting is not the way to solve problems, and we, as parents, did the same. In fact, it was something stressed in our family mainly because five boys in a household presented far too many opportunities to settle problems with fisticuffs rather then in a more civilized fashion.

By and large, the boys cooperated with our ban on socking each other. It actually surprised us that they got along as well as they did—at least most of the time. Part of the solution was that we kept them so busy they didn't have time to fight. The rest may have been simply that we constantly stressed talking things out rather than attacking each other.

Number four son, Robb, was probably the least attracted to physically aggressive tendencies. He preferred reading books and playing the piano to rolling around in the dust and dirt. Even in his many Scouting ventures over the years, his least favorite activities were hiking and camping. Robb was the one who would rather stay home and work on Citizenship in the Community or a Music Merit Badge. However, he did participate in the entire Boy Scout program. He knew that a Scout has to do it all, if he is to earn the Eagle rank, and all our boys felt this was a worthwhile goal they all eventually achieved.

Given Robb's personality, it was strange to us that it was he who would wind up getting into the most terrible fight of any of our boys. It was the most terrible because, to our knowledge, it was the only real fight where one of our boys wound up badly hurting someone else.

Having gone into the milieu of seventh grade, Robb, at age 12, and another boy he hardly knew began taunting and goading each other—both seeming bent on confrontation. Name calling and ugly words increased between the two until a "showdown" eventually seemed inevitable.

In the meantime, Robb one day performed a small act of simple courtesy that led to some wonderful and exciting experiences for him.

A piece of paper fell from his friend's notebook—a girl named Jenny Juhl. Robb quickly bent down and picked it up for her. He noted it was a short newspaper article, and the title "Peace Prize Contest" interested him.

"What's this about?" he asked Jenny.

"Oh, it's an article my mom gave me," she said. "I know you always do better writing essays than I do in English class. Why don't you just keep it? I don't plan to enter the contest anyway."

Robb thanked her as the bell rang, and they both hurried their separate ways.

Coming home that day, he read the article to me in the kitchen. It dealt with a Children's Peace Prize that was being offered to students, grades 4-8, for writing about their thoughts on world peace.

"The essays have to be in San Francisco in two days," he said. "I could win some money, and all I would have to do is write 500 words. I think I'll give it a try."

Not certain he could write something and get it sent off so quickly, I nevertheless encouraged him to give it a go.

Saying "Hello" to an opportunity, Robb enthusiastically dashed off to our newly acquired word processor and began his hunt and peck method of typing. About two hours later, he emerged with an essay on his feelings for achieving peace in the world. It began with a definition of the word that he had looked up in Webster's, and it emphasized how he felt children could lead the way in the effort to accomplish peace. It was a well-written composition for one so young.

A few hours later, Robb showed his work to his dad who said, "It isn't likely this will get to the place in time, but we'll mail it and see."

Dean took the essay to the post office that evening for Robb. At the time overnight service and fax machines were not a common option.

Robb, meanwhile, returned to school next day and again fell into the same jarring unpleasantness with his adversary. The jeers, and slurs, and dares, and taunts continued until Robb did the totally unexpected. He said to the kid one morning, "Okay, let's meet at LeGette Field after school."

Our young son, at the time, appeared thin and frail, but he was tougher and wirier than he looked. He had been involved in many friendly wrestling matches at home with his brothers—a few even not so friendly. He also played baseball, swam, and did some running. Even with all of this, few, even in his own family, would have bet odds on him in a serious physical entanglement.

I worried when he was almost a half-hour late getting home from school that afternoon. When he did come in, he looked horrible. He was dirty, scratched, hair a mess, face beet-red and sweaty, the knees of his pants split and stained with grass.

He looked at me without uttering a word, as I said to him, "What in the world happened to you?"

Then everything spilled out—what had been going on for weeks, his finally proposing a fight, and the results of the battle.

"I broke his arm," Robb said and then burst into tears. All the frustration and futility of what had happened came pouring out of him.

"I didn't really want to fight him," he cried. "I didn't want to hurt him."

He put his head against my arm, and I quietly gave him a hug and told him it was going to be okay.

"Go get a shower, and you'll feel much better," I suggested.

Later we talked more about the results of fighting, and Robb vowed he would do his best never to get involved in such a conflict again. I felt certain he never would.

Both boys were, however, suspended for a day when school officials got word of the fight. As one of the two sets of parents involved, Dean and I fully supported the school in the disciplinary action.

The day after the suspension, a thrilling call came to our home from San Francisco. Over five thousand California students had entered the Peace Prize Contest, and seven regional area winners had been selected.

"Your son, Robert, is our Sacramento area winner," the person on the phone said. "He will be awarded $1,000 by Mrs. Anwar Sadat of Egypt. The ceremony will be held in the Rotunda of the San Francisco City Hall in two weeks. Can one or both parents and Robert be there for the ceremony?"

As the impact of the message sunk in, the whole family just about fell off their collective chairs. Could this have happened to someone in our crowd?

As it turned out, both Dean and I and Robb were able to go to San Francisco. We were hosted overnight in a beautiful hotel and had the excitement of seeing the lovely and sophisticated Mrs. Sadat give Robb and each of the other winners a kiss, a check for $1,000, and a crystal sculpture. This ceremony was followed by a superb luncheon.

After arriving back home, Robb decided to share a portion of his winnings with each of his brothers. The rest he disposed of wisely, with a little encouragement from Mom and Dad, mostly into a savings account.

Our son learned many lessons that eventful weekend and, just by observing all that transpired, so did the rest of us.

Over the years, the irony and incongruity of Robb getting involved in a nasty fight, then winning a fabulous peace prize—all within a day or two—has remained a source of amusement for the entire family.

THE REAL WINNER

It may seem obvious to say that each child in a family is so very different, but how strikingly true this can be. Parents with only one child probably have a difficult time comprehending this concept. Those with two or more seem to be constantly amazed at the variations in character, looks, and personalities that can belong in one family.

So it was with each of our sons.

Four years after Glenn joined our family, we said, "Hello" to our second boy, Matthew, on a chilly February 19, in San Luis Obispo, California's Sierra Vista Hospital—three long, uncomfortable weeks after our family doctor said the baby would arrive the last weekend in January. Not having been sure of our date of conception, old Doc Smith was not anxious to induce labor, so when Matthew finally did arrive, he was long overdue, weighing ten pounds and a whopping 23 inches long—a big baby by any standards.

He had to be pushed by Doc Smith from the pelvic area into the birth canal, and it was not a simple birth. I had been given gas as an anesthetic and was not aware of the circumstances until afterwards.

Our baby appeared healthy and normal and started sleeping through the night at two weeks of age. What parents could complain about that? Pleasant and easy-going, he was all we could ask for in a wee one.

Matthew was late crawling, and Dean was the one who noticed that when he finally did go on all fours, his left hand did not seem to position itself correctly as he moved across the floor. I had not noticed the problem, however, and assumed that all was completely well with our husky, little boy.

However, once Dean made the observation, the two of us took Matthew to our doctor who immediately recommended we see a neurological specialist. We did so, and the astute, young physician examined Matthew carefully. He recommended an angiogram, a surgical procedure that required an overnight visit in the hospital. We, of course, anxiously waited for the results.

Next morning, the specialist gave his findings to us in a guarded and kindly way. Our little boy, the specialist said, had likely been deprived of oxygen at birth and would live his life with a mild case of cerebral palsy affecting mainly the left side of his body. We were told our son would probably not get any better nor any worse and that we were fortunate his physical limitation was not more severe than it was. We were greatly relieved to learn he would not be affected mentally by his handicap.

As time went on, we came to understand that challenges lay ahead as Matthew grew. The two of us did our best to meet these challenges, and we did our utmost to help Matthew do so as well. However, we were to learn this would not be easy.

Children who have not been taught to be kind and tolerant of others who are "different" can be incredibly cruel at times and, during Matthew's elementary school years, a few of these children hurt our son deeply. As he grew, Matthew developed a great relationship with his older brother and his three younger ones. He liked nothing better than to run and play with them and with his close friends, some of whom became life-long friends.

Nevertheless, during the elementary grades, careless children would call out, "Hey, Matt, how come you run crooked?" and other hurtful remarks.

This son, with his kind and gentle personality, just let these unfortunate comments and questions go by. The sting was there, but he never retaliated nor did he let show the pain they caused. He just carried on.

At the tender age of six, Matthew did ask us, after school one day, "What should I say when the kids ask me what's wrong with my arm and leg?"

We suggested he simply tell these children that he had a "motor control problem." We hoped that would give a brief explanation, perhaps puzzle the kids a bit, and put off further questions.

Next day, we asked Matthew how things went at school and what he had told the kids about his problem.

We had to laugh when our little guy replied, "They didn't say anything. I just told 'em I had a 'problem with my engine.'"

That explanation, we figured, probably put the taunters off just as well as the original one we had suggested—perhaps more so.

As time went on, we were to learn this boy of ours possessed a certain resoluteness that made him overcome adversity time and time again. We often called him our little mongoose. Anyone who has read Kipling's "Rikki-Tikki-Tavi" knows about the battle between the mongoose and the cobra. Though a fraction of the size of the huge East Indian serpent, the tiny mongoose can get a death grip on the throat of its victim, hanging on tenaciously until the serpent is dead.

Matthew was like that. Once he set his mind to something, he would hang on "come hell or high water," as his dad would say. Throughout his school years and beyond, he would take on a task and quietly see it to the finish no matter how hard it might be.

Just one example from his earlier years tells the tale:

Many children, faced with a physical challenge such as our son's, might simply refuse to participate in games and contests with their peers. Matt, however, was used to competitive activities with his brothers. The five of them would play all kinds of games and sports in our yard, mostly organized by their oldest brother, Glenn—football, basketball, and whatever. Perhaps this aided Matthew in not being afraid to participate with equal fervency in his school and Scouting endeavors.

How vividly I remember a scene from his Cub Scout days. At age eight, a Cub starts out as a Wolf Scout for a year, then a Bear Scout at nine, then a year as a Webelo before starting into the full-fledged Boy Scout organization when he's eleven.

Annual Olympics are held in all three years of the Cub Scouting program, and Matthew never failed to participate. However, the various races are often highly competitive, and Matt invariably came in last. As his parents, we always cheered him on at these events, but our hearts silently ached for him. However, Matthew seemed to give little care to where he placed in the competition. He just reveled in the fun of it all.

Glenn Sharp, Matthew's Scout leader, stood by our sides the final year of the Olympics. The familiar scenario repeated itself once again. There was Matthew doing his best, then standing on the sidelines, cheering for his buddies as they took their turns in the various events.

The time came, as usual, for the awards to be presented, and the First, Second, and Third place winners all came to walk away with their prizes. Matt again, also as usual, stood watching and appearing quite content in having had the fun of simply participating. He applauded for all of his buddies as they came forward to accept their awards.

Glenn Sharp, standing beside us, leaned over and quietly said, "You and I know who the *real* winner is here today."

And so our dear, sweet Matthew was ... and so he has continued to be ...

—on through his high school years where major surgery, performed to transfer tendons on his left leg, was only minimally successful in helping to correct his walk,

—on through college where he labored hard to earn a Master's Degree in Business Administration; it was not an easy go,

—on to marry a lovely girl he met in college who earned her own degrees in Nursing and Psychology,

—on to father five strong, healthy children,

—on to earn a good living and do his best to set an example for his own family to follow,

—on to continue to deal with nagging back and leg pain throughout his life because of the misalignment of his spine—pain of which he seldom speaks,

—on to live life with a funny and wry sense of humor

—on to teach us much about what the race of life is all about,

—on our Matthew continues to be ...

A WINNER!

C.A.Y.G.

◆

Try a Secret from McDonald's

It may be true that the kitchen is the heart of the home, but, until I learned a secret from the biggest of the "fast fooders," the heart of my home always looked like it had just suffered a major coronary. In fact, our whole family felt like moving to another house rather than trying to clean the mess. It wasn't that we didn't like a clean kitchen; it just seemed impossible to ever get it that way and keep it that way.

Then everything changed when our oldest son, Glenn, at the start of his school year decided to check out a job at McDonald's. He was 16 and needed some extra income. The same day he applied, he breezed through the door saying, "Hi, Mom. Guess what? I got the job!"

Working hard, just before Thanksgiving, he was promoted to a manager's position.

When the holiday rolled around at our house, I was doing my usual preparation for the big meal, along with some help from my husband and the kids. We all liked cooking but never seemed to get ahead of the clutter we created in the kitchen.

When the tasty meal was over and we'd filled ourselves with the done-to-perfection turkey and all the other goodies, we walked from our dining room into the kitchen and looked at the mountain of dirty dishes and pots and pans.

"Oh, no," was the thought in everyone's mind.

The second thought was that we ought to quietly walk away and maybe wait till closer to Christmas to attack the chaos.

Then Glenn said, "You know, what we need here is C.A.Y.G."

We all looked at him like he was from M.A.R.S.

"Okay," his younger brother said, "What's C.A.Y.G.? Does it have something to do with letting the cat clean up the mess?"

"Nope," said Glenn "C.A.Y.G. is something employees are taught when they first start training at McDonald's. It's how McDonald's got its reputation for being one of the cleanest and neatest of the fast food restaurants."

"So, what does it mean? How do they do it?" I asked, eager to implement anything to solve our on-going dilemma and seriously wanting "clutter to have its last stand" in our kitchen—words borrowed from the title of a household cleaning book I knew about titled *Clutter's Last Stand* by our friend, Don Aslett. I was all too well aware that mess makes stress, and I knew we would all be better off with less stress in our busy lives.

Glenn went on to tell us that McDonald's slogan, or acronym, simply means CLEAN AS YOU GO.

"It's easy," he said. "First, you start off with a clean work area. If it's not clean, you get it in shape enough so you have a fresh place to begin. Then all you do is keep some hot, soapy water in the sink, and every time you dirty a dish or a pan, you wash it, drain it, dry it, and put it away—or you stick it immediately in the dishwasher. As you prepare things on the counters, you wipe up your spills. You clean up each mess as soon as it happens."

Was this coming from the son whose bedroom was the only other disaster area in the house?

"But," I thought, "why not give it a try?" And so we did.

Obviously, it's never easy to change habits, but the whole family seemed to catch onto the need to put CAYG into practice—at least most of the time. As each of us made a mess, we thought CAYG, and we started cleaning as we went along.

We quickly realized we were saving a lot of time: no more food dried on the pots and pans, no more soaking time to get it off, kitchen implements clean and in place when we needed them, sink no longer piled high with dishes, floor swept and mopped as needed—the whole kitchen suddenly clean and organized. The change was amazing.

CAYG became a slogan around the entire house. The process carried over into the bedrooms where clothes were put on hangers instead of being dropped on the floor. In fact, throughout the house, nothing wound up on the floors which went a long ways toward making our abode appear much neater. We each took on a share of cleaning the bathrooms; we dusted and vacuumed regularly, thus staying ahead of the normal household dirt.

Stress lessened, and we all felt much better about living in a house of order.

Now, even though daily clutter still tries to rear its ugly head, we know how to attack it, keep thing organized, and get on with more important things in our lives. Thanks to our son sharing his secret from the Golden Arches, our family has a lot less mess and a lot more fun.

Re-written from an article titled "C.A.Y.G." published in *Good Housekeeping* magazine and subsequently reprinted in England's equivalent of the New York magazine.

GLENN AND THE ORANGE HAIR OR "I DID IT"

Sounds like the title of an old, comedic melodrama, and that's appropriate because raising kids is a melodrama, of sorts.

"Kids do the darndest things," Art Linkletter used to say, and there probably isn't a parent who would not agree. As an addendum to that thought, another wise person once counseled, "Never say, 'My child will never do this or that,' because you may just have to eat your words.'"

Surprises are definitely the order of the day when raising young 'uns. Obviously, with five sons, we had our share—both of the positive and the negative variety. Parents simply have to accept and adjust to these inevitable surprises and learning experiences in the child-rearing process.

Somehow, the oldest child seems to give parents the most surprises. Many psychologists say that parents tend to be harder on the oldest, too, and that has an impact on that particular child—again both positively and negatively.

Glenn, our oldest, gave us a few fits now and again and definitely tested our mettle as parents—nothing major, but enough to give us some challenges as he grew to manhood. He also often amazed us with his focused sense of right and wrong.

To wit, a couple of incidents come to mind that occurred during his teenage years—one involving a curfew hour and the other involving Glenn's hair, of all things. They are representative of both positive and negative surprises.

As to the curfew hour, it became readily apparent to us that children not only learn from their parents, but vice versa. Child rearing is, without question, a reciprocal school.

Imposing curfews is one of those areas that can work well toward its intended aims, or it can backfire, as we came to learn. From age 13 to 17, our oldest was happy to respect a reasonable hour that we set for him. The hour increased from 8 p.m. to 10 p.m. as he grew.

When he hit 17, we extended the hour to eleven o'clock, and that's when friction began to develop. We would be waiting for him at the appointed hour, and when he was more than a few minutes late, there would be trouble. The problem escalated to the point that it was creating all kinds of strife. Weeks and months went by with the same scenario of conflict occurring over and over again and no resolution in sight.

Maintaining our hard line, we took away privileges, and unhappiness for him and for us was the repeated result. We felt at a loss as to how to resolve the problem.

Then one night, Glenn came home his usual 10-15 minutes or so past eleven. We waited before we said anything and just looked at him. He took a deep breath and said to us, "Can we talk about this?"

We agreed it was definitely time to do just that, and we decided to listen to our son first, rather than starting to talk ourselves as we normally did.

"Let's hear what you have to say," his father said.

"Okay, he replied, "I don't know if you realize it or not, but I'm becoming an adult."

We thought about that and realized it was true.

"Lots of times after a game or whatever," he continued, "I'm with a group of friends, and we're in the middle of a conversation about something important, and I feel awkward saying, 'I gotta go.' I feel under a lot of pressure when I know I'm supposed to be home right on the dot."

We could understand that. His feelings, we acknowledged to ourselves, were part of the maturing process, and he was explaining them well.

He continued, almost pleading, "Why don't you just trust me that I'll do my best to be home as close to the time as I can? Usually I'm not more than a few minutes late, but I would like to be able to use my own judgement. If I'm going to be later than usual, I'll do my best to give you a call. Otherwise, I'll be home close to eleven or shortly after. I promise I won't abuse the privilege. That way I can be a lot more relaxed, and you can too."

His simple logic was difficult to refute. It left us without much to say in return. We told our son we would think about what he had said and let him know our feelings. The problem on our part, we began to realize, was the business of cutting the apron strings, and somewhat reluctantly we decided to give our son's suggestion a try.

"Glenn," we said the next day. "Since you feel more like an adult, we have decided to treat you more like an adult. We feel, as you said, that this is a matter of trust, and we'll give your idea a try with that in mind."

To our amazement, the plan worked flawlessly. If anything, Glenn was late less often than he had been in the past and, if he did have a problem, he was great about calling to let us know. He was visibly less tense, and so were we—just one of many lessons the two of us learned in the "give and take" of being parents.

Our oldest son surprised us again the year he graduated from high school. After talking his plans over with us, he decided to spend the summer on the island of Maui in Hawaii before heading off to college—not vacationing—but working on a pineapple plantation. It sounded exotic and interesting, and we decided it would likely be a good experience for him.

Little did we realize that summer would involve the hardest work he would probably ever do, as well as a life-threatening situation.

We said our first major "goodbye" to our son, seeing him off early in June with a pang in our hearts—but knowing the absence would only be for three months. And we were lucky enough to arrange a trip to the islands ourselves toward the end of his stay to see him and to take a long overdue vacation ourselves.

When we arrived on Maui in August, we hardly recognized the hulk of a young man who greeted us. Glenn not only appeared taller, tanned, and much more muscular after his months in the fields—he shocked us with a head of bright, orange hair! (This was in the days prior to the punk rock look of dyed and spiked hairdos.)

"What's this?" we cried as we hugged him and rubbed his strange looking hair with our hands.

He laughed and said, rather sheepishly, "My buddy and I both had some great tans to go home with, but because of the hats we had to wear, we couldn't get the sun-bleached look in our hair that some of the guys had, so we tried a little hair color to get the effect—and it turned orange!"

We just shook our heads. Did we really know this pumpkin head or carrot top? Did we want to know him? We wondered.

Glenn, meanwhile, hosted us remarkably well during our brief visit to the plantation. For a few minutes, he let his dad take a turn behind the huge boom, as the pineapple harvester is called. The work, even after fifteen minutes, was grueling. Wearing leather chaps and arm covers, Glenn showed how he had to bend and snap off each individual pineapple, often weighing ten pounds or more, then swing his body up and around, tossing the fruit onto the boom, all the while walking through a tangle of huge pineapple plants with their sharp-edged leaves.

In the oppressive, tropical heat, this work went on for three eight-hour shifts. Thick gloves were worn, but at one point a spear from one of the plants pierced Glenn's arm, and he developed blood poisoning. Thankfully, quick medical care prevented any major problems.

Glenn told us that it was not uncommon for the crew of teenagers to try to sabotage the efforts of the work from time to time just to get a break. They became adept at seeing who could devise the most creative method for affording themselves more frequent rests than were allotted. It became a game of sorts—one which the supervisors understood and usually tolerated, even though grudgingly.

He went on to tell us about an incident that occurred one day when a nail was strategically placed in the path of the boom truck. One of the big tires went over it, and a hiss of air could be heard escaping. This, obviously, shut everything down completely—much to the delight of the young workers. The supervisor, known by the boys as the luna (or the 'big kahuna'), was more than a little upset.

"Okay, you guys, this time you've gone too far. I want to know who did this."

The game suddenly was no longer a game, and faces grew serious.

"I repeat," he said, "I want to know the person who blew the tire."

Sixteen young men looked at each other for a long minute—and then at the boss.

"I did it."

The words came from Glenn, and the supervisor looked visibly shocked.

"Okay, Glenn, you and I need to talk." The luna pulled Glenn aside.

Our son's reputation as a hard worker had been excellent, and he immediately felt badly about a prank that he realized had gone way too far. Embarrassed about the incident, he apologized sincerely. Fortunately for Glenn, the supervisor reprimanded him only lightly, then directed him to help with the repair and get on with the job.

"I like your honesty," he told Glenn. "I like a man who can 'own up' when he does something that isn't right. I'll give you another chance to prove yourself, Glenn."

And prove himself Glenn did. Before the summer ended, he became an assistant to the luna and, at the end of August, he felt good about finishing an incredibly difficult job. This was especially true since a number of other young men had long since quit and left for home—paying their own way back, which was part of the contract.

Once again, in an unusual situation far from home, we, as Glenn's parents, found ourselves learning something important. By watching our son and listening to him, we witnessed how he, as a developing adult, was learning to deal with life and its many challenges.

THE MAN OUR SON NOW IS

One day it's all over. The thought comes almost like a blazing revelation.

"Our job is done. Our son is grown and doesn't need us anymore."

Parenting is, in reality, a job where you know you have succeeded when you have successfully worked yourself out of a job—that job having been to carefully guide a child and then slowly let go.

In some ways the above statements are really not completely true, however. Yet, at the same time, they are. It's a paradox. Your job *is* done—at least in the larger sense. There are no more diapers and bottles, no more school papers, no more dating days, no more sports and school activities, no more meals and laundry. Yet, in another sense, because you are a parent, you will always be on the job.

As one mother put it, "I only now realize the magnitude of it all. What I did or didn't do will affect her all her life. I cannot go back and redo any of it, and I can only hope that the mistakes I made on days I was too busy or out-of-sorts and angry were balanced by the times I set everything aside to give her the attention needed. Her father and I have no choice now except to perform the final act of good parenting: letting her go. Our hearts and our house have empty rooms now. But our offspring will carry with her the indelible imprint of our home life together. This imprint is so enduring that some of it will be passed on to her children—and to her children's children."

All of this I believe to be true ... and quite sobering.

Since Dean and I raised only sons, we now have to stand back, as all parents do, and try to take an objective look at these young men we have raised. If we have done our job well, and if they have heeded the best of the counsel we gave, they will be able now to stand on their own. It is our hope and prayer that they will carry on the best of the teachings and patterns we have set for them (given our own imperfections, of course, as bumbling human beings).

Dean is the one who always says, "Don't look back—not at this stage of the game—at least not to things done wrong or mistakes made."

Good advice.

He has persuaded me that it's best to look back only as I remember each son in turn—the smell of that freshly bathed baby, the dimples at the base of each chubby finger, the tiny toes, and the angel-soft hair. It's fun to remember his first steps, then walking along, his hand in mine, and later the scraped knees, the worn-out jeans, the baseball hat, and the sweaty brow. I like to recall the fun of bedtime kisses and hugs, reading together his first books, the squeals of joy and the tears we helped brush away. I think of high school days, and hairy legs and a deepening voice, then the major turning point of graduation day.

Then, as a mother, it's also time for me to execute my own turning point, as I look ahead from this time on. I have to trust that I, along with his father, have given him what he needs to meet the world and its tremendous challenges head-on.

In mind's eye, as I watch my son go on life's way, I often want to give him a big hug and a kiss and tell him how proud I am of him for measuring up to life's struggles and striving each day to do the best he can. I also want to tell him how very, very much I love him—this very special son of mine—this boy who is now a man.

Excerpted from the book *Boy, Oh, Boy: Boy-raising Secrets Every Parent Should Know* by Dean & Nancy Hoch, Horizon Publishers, 1990.

LETTER TO A SON ON THE EVE OF HIS MARRIAGE

Dear Son,

When you phoned us last week to say you were planning to get married it was a bit of a shock. There had been indications, of course, but still we were somehow unprepared. You seemed so anxious for this big step, but we don't feel quite that ready.

After you hung up, we sat and looked at each other. What do parents do at this time in their lives? We've always said we would voice any objections we might have beforehand and then do our best never to say anything critical afterward. And since we have no objections, we came to the conclusion that all we need to do now is simply to "let go." Yet, because we love you so much, that isn't easy to do.

We ask ourselves, "Have we done our best to prepare you for this crucial time in your life?" And feelings of inadequacy hit us squarely in the face as we ask the question.

We realize that you have watched our example—how we have treated each other—since you were a child. What you have seen has carried a clearer message than anything we could possibly say now. We hope you will remember our kisses and hugs in the kitchen, our occasional week-end dates, and the inevitable marital confrontations which we did our best to settle quickly or hide from you. Most of all, we hope that somehow the love we have for each other, and the trust we have always placed in each other, will have touched your life in a way that will carry over into your own marriage.

You're a man now, but for just a little while longer we would like to exercise our parenting prerogative and give you some important thoughts as you prepare to "tie the knot." Once this advice is given, we plan to get out of the advice business and do our best to stay out. You probably already know much of what we have to say; however, we feel this is a good time to restate a few facts. Some of this may seem old-fashioned, as you would say. But we have learned, sometimes the hard way, that many old-fashioned principles do bring much happiness. So as you establish your own home, please remember:

• <u>Marriage is no easy business</u>. It's one of life's most difficult and most challenging "schools." It can also be life's supreme joy when two unselfish people give themselves to each other. Remember that, even though it may appear so now, no one is perfect. You are not, and neither is the girl you have chosen for your own. As the saying goes, "Keep your eyes wide open before marriage and half shut afterward." Recognize that everyone has his or her faults, and that it's unwise to dwell on them. Concentrate on the good things instead.

• <u>If you feel you are prepared for marriage, make sure you have the financial means to see it through</u>. We have supported you to this point in your life. Now you must stand on your own two feet. After much careful consideration, we have established a policy not to give financial assistance to our married children. We have watched parents give their married children money to buy a new car or other major purchases. In almost all cases, such help seems to undermine rather than strengthen a marriage. So, unless something such as a major medical emergency arises, be prepared to enjoy the challenge—and the satisfaction—of providing for your own household.

• <u>Don't feel you can start out at the same level it took your parents more than 20 years to reach</u>. Be content with living in a modest apartment or a small house. Buy your furniture and appliances only when your finances allow. Use your dollars wisely and realize the joy in gradually raising your standard of living as your means permit. Pull together to accomplish your goals, and this, too, will strengthen your marriage.

• <u>Never strike or abuse each other in any way</u>. This probably seems unthinkable right now. However, many young couples, especially in the early years of marriage, become frustrated. It is, after all, a period of major adjustment. So, when anger surfaces, leave the room or the house for a while, if need be. Do what you need to do to cool off, but never do something in a moment of anger which you will regret later on.

• <u>The world is full of opportunities to cheat</u> on your partner. Keep clear of places where the opportunity exists. Be ever wary of even the beginnings of a desire in this direction. Never look twice at an attractive member of the opposite sex, especially in a provocative situation. Build your marriage on mutual trust—you toward your wife and she toward you.

• <u>Make every effort to see that your spouse experiences the same joy and fulfillment in your marriage as you do yourself</u>. This will take time and caring on your part, but it will draw you both closer together and make your marriage a happy one. Sometimes all either of you will want is a hug or a caring glance. Don't be afraid to sacrifice your own wants and wishes to make your partner happy. Be sensitive to each other's needs, and your marriage will benefit greatly.

• <u>Build your home on a strong foundation</u>. Make it a habit to worship together each week, and don't put off having your family. Children are a special joy and draw a couple together. Also, plan so that one of you is always with your little ones. This may mean Mom having to put off career plans for a few years. However, this will be a sacrifice well worth making; it will help build a strong home and a strong family.

• <u>Once you make this most important decision to marry, treat it as one that will last forever</u>. When the going gets rough, don't think about trotting back home. Be willing to steer your ship through the rough waters as well as the smooth. When things hit bottom, which happens now and again in every marriage, never give up—never. Make it your goal to work as hard as you can to make your marriage as rich and wonderful as it can possibly be.

Well, Son, we've said enough. With these words of counsel, our job as your mom and dad is almost finished. In spite of our faults and imperfections, we have made every effort to raise you the best we knew how. Though the road for us has been difficult at times, as it will be for you, the rewards of holding a marriage and a family together are more than you can ever imagine. We hope the same joy we feel now will be yours one day.

Our blessings go with you always.

With deepest love and caring,
Mother & Dad

Previously published in ***These Times*** magazine.

THE DAY WE PRUNED THE ROSES

Much is written and said about the touchy subject of abortion. As with any heated debate, arguments rage, and polarization seems difficult to prevent.

All parents who face this decision must do so as their own background, values, and consciences dictate. The choice is probably never an easy one to make. It was one I had to face.

◆   ◆   ◆

"Hey, Mom," our 18-year old, Greg, said. "If we're going to get that garden work done, we'd better get busy. I have to be at basketball practice at two o'clock."

"Okay, I really do appreciate your help," I replied, as we grabbed some trash bags, gloves, a pair of clippers, and headed for the back yard. "With both of us working, this shouldn't take very long," I said.

This late November day in Southeast Idaho was unseasonably warm. Greg had been swamped with the activities of his Senior year of high school, including sports, drama, music, and serving as the school's newly-elected Student Body President. I, too, had been busy taking some classes at nearby Idaho State University and had not begun the job of preparing our rose garden for the winter.

As I looked at Greg, I wondered how I could be so fortunate as to have a son this age actually willing to take the time to help me prune a whole fence row of bushes. For most kids his age, I knew it would be a boring chore. I wondered what it was that made him seem almost anxious to help me with this task. Perhaps he was thinking, as I was, that he would be leaving for college soon and that our time together was growing short.

This youngest of our five, Greg, like his brothers, was tall and handsome. With clear blue eyes and neatly cut brown hair, he appeared unassuming, yet exuded energy and talent. With a great sense of humor, he was a special individual to his family and to a wide circle of friends.

"I'll prune, and you hold the bag, Mom," he suggested.

As we worked, I quietly remarked to Greg, "You know, tending a garden is like raising and caring for a family—lots of time and effort."

Too young to fully understand, he just said, "Yep."

We chatted briefly as we worked. However, I felt that both of us sensed the sharing of the enjoyment of our task and of our love for each other. As we continued to clip and load the bags, my thoughts went back to a doctor's office many years earlier—before any of our children were born.

"Nancy, you might as well tell your fiancé it's almost certain you'll never have any children," our old family doctor told me. He also spoke with Dean about the situation.

Dean simply responded, "It doesn't matter. If need be, we'll adopt our family."

I spent much of the first three years of our marriage seeing a fertility specialist in Pittsburgh hoping to prove that doctor wrong. The procedures ended in my having major surgery on my ovaries, and I was finally able to conceive.

Following our move to San Luis Obispo, California, Glenn was born on the first day of spring. Our joy was complete. Both of us took so much delight in that dear little boy.

Though we hoped for another child, it was four years before Matthew joined our family. As his name means, to us he was another "gift of God." We couldn't have enjoyed him more.

Shortly after Matthew's birth, the four of us moved to Berkeley, California, and Dean began work on a Doctor's degree in education. Matthew was only a year old when we found we were expecting again.

"Where's that doc who said we'd never have any kids?" Dean joked.

We both had the feeling our family was now coming a little too fast. However, the addition of our Christmas baby, Barry, was something quite wonderful in our lives. At his birth, Dean rushed out and bought him a tiny Santa Claus outfit, and Barry was the delight of the entire maternity wing at the hospital—and of everyone at home, too. He fit right into the family circle, and Dean and I marveled at how our love could expand to include each new child.

We did realize, however, that some active family planning would have to be instituted if Dean were to be able to continue to pursue his studies. In spite of our efforts, however, less than two years later, our "Fourth of July" baby, Robert, made his entrance on the scene.

This newest addition was quite the "corker." He kept us up half the night for seven months and pulled such antics as scooting his crib close enough to his dresser to grab the container of baby powder and shake its contents all over himself and the entire bedroom. And that was just for starters. Once during a nap, he reached into a messy diaper and decorated his entire crib as well as the bedroom wall with the contents—also his hair, nose, and the intricately carved wooden dowels on his bed—all to be discovered by Mother two hours later. Uggh!

In spite of these and other trials, Robbie was a smart little cutie, and we obviously wouldn't have traded him for "all the gold and silver in the whole world" … as we told each of our boys when they were small.

"You wouldn't?" each would say. It was a concept that seemed to amaze them. (We didn't add that we wouldn't have given a nickel for another one—at least not right at the moment.)

Dean and I had wanted a family, and we were definitely getting what we wanted. At times, however, the work load and the challenges of four little boys, plus the pressures of schooling, seemed overwhelming. Dean often stayed home to help me when he should have been studying.

"Go on over to the library," I would say, and the reply would usually be, "Nope, you've had a hard day. I'll watch the boys while you take a walk or go shopping."

"But your grades will suffer," I would protest.

"I'd rather take a B or two," he typically replied and then, with a twinkle in his eye, he would tack on his favorite expression, "After all—in the eternal scheme of things—what's really most important? Family, right?"

Both of us had made the commitment early on that our family would indeed come first in our lives. As with the marriage vows, however, the words were easy to say; the daily living of them was difficult indeed.

Then came some bigger problems. Complications following Robert's birth caused me to come close to a nervous breakdown, and this situation ushered in the most challenging period of our marriage—a frightening time for both of us. Medical efforts did not alleviate the problems; I was having severe panic attacks, and the cause was unknown.

All the while, I was nursing this fourth little boy, and Dean and I knew we had to be extra careful about adding any more children to the family at this time. However, in spite of using every method of birth control we knew, nature worked yet another of her surprises, and I found, with a seven-month old in my arms, that I was expecting again.

Neither of us could believe this turn of events.

One of Dean's major advisors at Berkeley called him into his office and bluntly said, "You'll never get through your degree if you keep producing kids instead of research. As it is, you're having to work more than half time, and your progress in the department is slow, to say the least. If you don't start going full time and get out of here, I will personally see you never get your degree from this institution."

These comments came just as Dean was seriously considering doing just that. I knew he was wondering how he could finish his degree with family and financial pressures mounting.

Knowing that this professor was going beyond the bounds of propriety, however, Dean fired back, "I'll have my family, I'll take care of them, and I *will* finish this degree as well."

As far as Dean was concerned, this professor had thrown down the gauntlet, and I, of course, was in total agreement with Dean. We both wanted the degree, and we were not about to give up now. So we re-doubled our efforts to accomplish the goal together—I, though not feeling well. I cared for the boys, typed papers for my husband and for other students as well to earn extra money. Dean, meanwhile, studied and worked hard at a part-time job to provide for us.

Meanwhile, I talked with an obstetrician at the Kaiser Permanente HMO in Richmond, near Berkeley, about our fifth baby, now on the way. Assessing my state of mental and physical weakness at the time, he took me off guard by quickly suggesting, "I think you should have an abortion."

The idea had never occurred to me until that moment. Then, in a matter of seconds, my mind traveled down a long, and dark, and dangerous road only to see that it ended in sadness and, for me, life-long remorse.

Again, in seconds, my mind traveled back to the stark, white walls of the examining room, facing the doctor who awaited my reply. Because of the way I had been raised and my own set of values, the decision was not really a decision at all.

"No, that won't be an option," I said—and to myself I reflected, "Life, I know, is just too precious to be terminated (whimsically or otherwise). This pregnancy and delivery may be hard, but I know I can get through it."

In my own way, I was every bit as tenacious as Dean. We both knew from experience that the strength comes to get through tough times—it simply comes. And often, once a difficult decision is made (sometimes very quickly), things often seem to simply work out much easier than anticipated.

It was so with this pregnancy. Happily for both of us, it turned out to be the easiest of the five. As it progressed, I gradually began to feel much better, and I was actually amazed that everything went so well. Part of it, I know, was the sheer determination Dean and I both had to make the best of things—another attitude both of us had been taught as children.

Greg, our last, was born November 5 on a wintry evening in Utah, where we had moved temporarily. What a delight this baby was to the two of us and his four older brothers. He seemed to be no trouble at all. The other boys played with him, and they all pitched in, along with their Dad, in helping with this new member of the family.

As I had done with each of his brothers, I nursed him and held him close to my heart—a quiet and special time—at least when the other four weren't racing and yelling around the house. Watching this last one grow, I often looked at him and thought, "What if this special boy had never been? What if I had chosen to end his chance for life?"

As it was, our "basketball team," as Dean called them, grew up almost without us being aware—or so it seemed. The task of raising all of them was obviously not an easy one, and we had our hard times, as all parents do. Nevertheless, the boys added a rich and wonderful dimension to our lives. Somehow, Dean and I felt that without each of them, a great void would have existed. Each seemed such a vital part of the two of us and of each other. And our last son—perhaps because he was our last—brought us an added measure of joy.

"Looks like we're about done, Mom," Greg said, bringing me back to reality.

"Yes," I replied, looking at him and then at the roses.

I couldn't help but compare the raising of this son and our others to the process Greg and I were now completing. Just as we pruned these roses, so Dean and I had to "prune" our boys—"cutting them down to size now and again," as Dean would say, with needed discipline and training. This was important, of course, so they would eventually shape into the kinds of human beings that could be a credit to the world … and they have.

As Greg and I pushed the remainder of the clippings into the bags, he looked at me and said, "How come we're so lucky to have such a neat family, Mom?"

Surprised by his question, I gazed into his eyes, realizing that he, too, had been doing some pondering himself as we worked. "Seems as though every day is important," he continued seriously. "Like you and Dad always say, 'We need to make each one special.'"

His words touched me. I looked at this wonderful boy who might never have had his turn on earth. How grateful I was for him and all he had become. How grateful I was that I had been raised in a home that taught me about the sanctity of life.

As the warm November sun shone on the two of us, I knew I would tuck this very special day away in my heart and remember it always ... the day we pruned the roses.

SAMPLES OF OUR SONS' WRITINGS

GERSHWIN TO GO

By
Robb Hoch

I was destined to be a Gershwin fan. While I was yet in the womb, my mom decided to try out some advice about playing music to unborn infants. Since one of her favorite composers was George Gershwin, I was quite familiar with his "Concerto in F," "An American in Paris," and a few others by the time the doctor spanked me. However, it wasn't until my Junior year in high school that George Gershwin really had an impact on me.

Though we lived in Pocatello, Idaho, one of the best piano teachers around taught at Utah State University in Logan, Utah. A series of unusual happenings landed me a tryout with him, and he agreed to take me on as a student. So twice a month for the next two years, one of my parents would pick me up after school, we would drive the hour and a half to my lesson, spend an hour there, grab a bite to eat, and drive the distance back (usually in time to get me to the high school dance.).

Throughout the trip we would talk and listen to either rock or classical music. My parents were understanding enough of my teenage interests to tolerate a good share of my tunes. It was usually my mom who suggested equal time for classical music. When classical time arrived, I automatically reached for the light classic, "Rhapsody in Blue." It became a tradition to listen to it at least once during the trip.

I can't really say what made the difference that February day, but Gershwin's "Rhapsody" captivated me as it never had before. Driving down that familiar two-lane highway with Mom, listening to Gershwin for the upteenth time, I became totally absorbed in the music. My faculties became heightened, and my senses became more acute. I breathed deeply, immersed in the exhilarating thrill of the music. That day I realized that good music would always be a source of peace and enjoyment, even ecstasy to me.

I glanced over at my mom, and things began to get blurry. I realized one day I would be a parent, trying to instill in my children similar feelings about music, hoping they would respond as I was responding. But more than that I hoped my children would love me like I loved my mom.

The tape ended as we pulled into the parking lot. I gave my mom a quick kiss, jumped out of the car, and walked toward the building. I looked back at her one more time before I went through the double doors.

I've looked back many times since.

Previously published in **The New Era** Magazine

Note: The following story represents what was almost a tragic "goodbye" to an entire family of dear ones.

Turn the Wheel! Turn It Now!

By
Glenn Hoch
(Now a father of five himself)

Heading to our family reunion at Bear Lake, Utah proved to be a much more exciting time for my wife, Debbie, myself, and our five children, ages 10 to one and a half, than we ever anticipated. Though we had recently been though some severe financial struggles, we had saved our pennies so we would be able to join my four brothers and their families, along with the grandparents of our growing clan. We looked forward to a weekend of recreation and renewal for all of us.

Traveling north from our home in Orem that Friday afternoon in mid-July, I began to get accustomed to driving the Jeep Cherokee that a neighbor insisted we use for the weekend. Everyone at the reunion was looking forward to taking rides in the motorboat we were towing behind the borrowed vehicle. We had owned our boat for several years and enjoyed the recreation it provided us and our extended family.

After nearly two hours on the road, our leisurely drive suddenly took a disappointing turn. As we headed up a steep hill leading to the south side of the Bear Lake area, the Cherokee completely lost its power, and we had to pull over to the side of the road.

Several cars whizzed by, and we were surprised and pleased when, within minutes, a pickup truck pulled to a stop in front of our vehicle. A young man got out and came back to ask if we were having problems. We noticed a young woman and a small girl in the truck with him. I explained that the motor on the Jeep had died, and he immediately offered to tow us to a service station.

Gratefully, I helped him secure the tow rope and felt relieved; however, my relief was short-lived. Immediately after cresting the top of the hill and starting down the other side, the power to the Cherokee's brakes failed.

With the sickening feeling that I had no control over the vehicle or the violently swaying boat behind it, I knew I had the choice of running into the pickup ahead of us, allowing the car to veer to the left down a steep ravine, or turning the wheel and making what I knew would be an extremely sharp and dangerous turn up over a hillside on the right hand side of the road.

As the Jeep gained nearly uncontrollable momentum, I distinctly heard a voice in my mind saying, "Turn the wheel! Turn it now!" Another thought flashed through my mind: "Just a few more yards, and the road turns. The lay of the land could be better there—more level—more secure."

A second time, the warning voice burned itself into my mind: "Turn the wheel! Turn it now!"

Having worked as a police offer, fireman, and paramedic, I had been in many frightening circumstances. However, I had never been more frightened in my life than I was at that moment.

I knew for a certainty that, if things went wrong, the sharp turn of the wheel would propel us all to our deaths. However, I felt urged to respond to the voice. I yanked the wheel to the right, spinning our car and boat up and over the rough incline. The speed of the Cherokee carried us bouncing and jostling over weeds, bumps, and perilous terrain.

As the car lurched, my wife and children screamed frantically, and I could do nothing but hang onto the wheel and guide the Cherokee and our careening boat to a stop some 30 yards or more after the turn.

All seven of us sat in the car in a state of near shock, our hearts pounding, our emotions raw. Within minutes the young man who had been driving the pickup found his way to us. Fortunately, the tow rope had snapped during the turn, and no damage had come to him or his passengers.

He immediately went to call for a tow truck, then returned to spend the next two and a half hours waiting with our family for the truck and then accompanying us to our destination at Bear Lake.

At the reunion site, my younger brother, Barry, discovered that a severely burned wire in the engine had caused the problem. He repaired it within a few hours but said it could have been a much more serious problem. We knew we were blessed to be alive.

Before the driver of the pickup went on his way, we learned that his wife, the other passenger in the car, was eight months pregnant and that their little daughter was only three. With that knowledge, I again felt sincere gratitude that no harm had come to his young family.

He told us that they never took that road to their home in Montpelier, Idaho. However, on that particular day, they decided to take a different route. How grateful we were that they did. And how thankful I was, too, that I had heeded the insistent voice directing me to turn the wheel and take my family and myself to safety.

A TIME FOR FRIENDS

BEING FRIENDLY AND ITS REWARDS ... JUST SAYING "HELLO"

There's something special about the simple act of smiling and saying "Hello." It's a rare person, indeed, who does not react favorably to a warm and friendly greeting.

From the time we are welcomed into this old world, scientists tell us that the warmth of a human voice is critical to our development. As we grow, it's just simply nice to hear our name attached to the brief but friendly and meaningful salutation of "Hi, there," or "Hello." This is true in virtually any language on earth.

As to the sheer practicality of saying "Hello," our family had the experience of moving to a new community as one of our sons was entering his Sophomore year of high school. Needless to say, he was not anxious to make a move at this time in his young life. In fact, the reluctance proved to be more than we had expected.

Understanding that our son exhibited a somewhat shy and reserved personality to this point in his life, we decided to counsel with him as to how to come out of himself and make the effort of projecting a whole new personality at his new school. Not easy to do, obviously, but we knew he had the capability to make this kind of change.

Our simple, but important, advice to him was as follows:

"Start out your very first day at this new school by learning the first name of every student you meet, as well as the names of your teachers and school administrators. Then every time you see that person again, smile and say 'Hi, Melissa,' or 'Hello, Dr. McWilliam,' or 'Howdy, Ryan.'"

We explained the fact that people like the sound of their name attached to a friendly greeting. We added, "Believe it or not, this little tidbit of advice really can make a huge difference, not just in school, but throughout your life."

We also told him some advice his great-grandmother always said, "To have friends, you have to be a friend."

The ending line of the story is that the following year, when Robb decided to run for student body president in his new school of over 1200 students, he won. Imagine that, after being so shy just a year before.

Winning a school election was never his motivation. He simply went beyond our advice of simply saying "Hello" to everyone. He reached out to every one of his classmates—kids that were known as "stoners" and "losers," as well as the "the popular kids," "the bookworms," and the "sports jocks." In so doing, he came to genuinely like just about every one of them, and they, obviously, came to like him as well. This all involved effort, of course, as well as a lot of memorization, but the effort proved so very worthwhile for everyone concerned.

Some years later, we shared this story with a shy, young girl we met. She had confided in us that she was fearful of going from junior high to high school.

Several years later, when we sent her a wedding gift, she replied with a thank you note that added: "You will never know how much your advice to me about smiling and saying 'Hello' to everyone I met—and also learning and using their names—meant to me; it changed my life ..."

Similarly, while still a young girl myself, I remember my father as a man who had a way of making the burdens of others lighter by following this same practice, including one particularly grumpy individual with whom he worked. Without fail, month after month, Dad would smile and say, "Hello, Jim," and Jim would rarely, if ever, respond. He would just go on his own negative way. Nevertheless, my father refused to let the coldness of his co-worker chill the brightness he naturally carried within himself.

Then one day, my dad—preoccupied with a serious family situation—neglected to offer his usual hearty "Hello" to Jim. A few hours later Jim surprised him by saying, "Hey, Bob, are you okay? I missed you saying 'Hello' to me this morning."

My dad often said that he "just about fell over" to think Jim had even noticed his reaching-out effort for such a very long time.

Throughout our lives, our family has found this very simple act of smiling and saying "Hello"—which takes so very little effort—is a good and enriching thing for all of us to do—an act and a gift, of sorts, that benefits us in ways we would never have guessed and also seems to make the world a better place in which to live.

THE BIG SWEDE

People come and go in our lives. Some we like; others we could do without. Still others—those rare and wonderful ones—make positive, indelible impressions on us, and our lives are forever changed for the better.

For our family, Don Mohr fit into the latter category. A 6' 6" Swede, Don radiated exuberance. Not only imposing in size, he was imposing in character and personality as well.

"Howdy, Governor," or "Hello there, Captain," would be a typical greeting he might shout to a male friend he hadn't seen for a while. To a lady, he would say, "Wonderful to see you, beautiful lady," or "Top of the morning to you, my dear."

He confided that these greetings were usually issued when he had forgotten someone's name. No matter. Whether he used your name or one of his favorite salutations, you simply felt happier and more important than you did the minute before Don's hand shook yours or he gave you a firm, friendly, squeeze around your shoulders.

Don married an equally effervescent sweetheart named Norma, also tall, and outgoing like himself. Together they produced seven daughters and two sons, all with their parent's blond-haired, blue-eyed, German/Scandinavian look.

All statuesque, like their parents, the offspring were among the most self-assured, self-confident, friendly, good-looking, and poised young people we ever met. Several of the six-foot tall daughters became beauty pageant queens, and all nine adored and respected their parents.

We asked ourselves, "How are these two parents raising such remarkable kids?" Because of that question, we spent the years we knew the family observing and trying to put into practice, with our own sons, much of what we were learning from them.

Don had some extraordinary ideas about life in general and about child-rearing in particular. As with any controversial-type personality, some people liked his unorthodox manners and ideas; a few others we knew disliked him passionately; some scoffed; some avoided; but the wise, we strongly believed, benefitted from what they observed, as did we.

At the outset Don shared with anyone who would listen his theme that, "Life is for experiences." It was one of his favorite expressions. If you were interested, he would tell you what he meant. His idea was simply that life is a school—a laboratory—an adventure—and, as he would say, "Why get in a rut? Why have the same experiences over and over again?" He meant this, particularly as it applied to earning a living, but he really intended the concept to expand to any area of life that could be confined within a moral and ethical framework.

Don had been educated as a teacher and engineer. He tried both professions for several years and then decided he wanted to open a jewelry store. This occupation, like the others, he operated until he tired of yet another venture.

By this period in his life, he and Norma had teenagers, so they decided to give the kids the experience of a family business—a bakery, no less. Buying the needed equipment, they installed it in the health department-approved back room of their home. Then all eleven of them arose each morning at 4 a.m. and baked big, delicious cinnamon rolls that became the rage of the suburban Sacramento area where they lived. The kids delivered the warm rolls to early morning business people before leaving for school.

The enterprise went on for a few years and served the purpose the parents intended—providing the kids with their spending money and, more importantly, teaching family work, family values, individual responsibility, and bonding. Easy to do? Hardly. Beneficial to the family? The tale told itself in their characters.

From this venture, Don went into a rug cleaning and window tinting business. This he and Norma continued to run after the kids left home. They both enjoyed the flexibility this kind of work offered, allowing them to leave on a trip whenever they wanted and also the independence of reporting to no one but themselves.

In all their various family activities, Don's philosophy of life played a major role. As each child grew, Don would tell them in his rapid-fire way, "I'll raise you and provide for you till you're 18; then it's out, out, out.... You make your own way after that" ... and they did.

One of the sons, unfortunately, didn't get the message right away and, on his 18th birthday, he found all his belongings stacked on the front porch.

The concept sounds harsh but, in addition to plenty of tough love, Don gave his kids the kind of practical education that allowed them to face the world at this young age and even earlier.

For example, television was never a part of their growing up lives; a set was not allowed in the house. Instead, constant activity prevailed, including experimentation, hobby development, and plenty of lively kinds of caring. Besides school, there was church involvement, Scouting, and any other endeavor the parents felt to be of value.

Photography, for example, was one of the prized family hobbies, and huge, blown-up photos of the individual kids and of family groupings decorated all the walls of their home. What children wouldn't feel elated to see themselves tossing a ball, or blowing up a balloon, or reading a book in life-size enlargements?

The modest Mohr home, itself, comprised a heavily-used entry way into a small kitchen. This, in turn, led to a small sitting area and then to a converted, double-car garage that formed an immense family room. A total of only three bedrooms and one small bath flanked the main rooms, and the nine kids shared their cramped quarters with few, if any, complaints.

For the many family birthdays, friends and neighbors were informally invited to come into the big family room and participate in a lively celebration. "Hooray, hurrah, Hiroshima" (with the emphasis on the "o" of Hiroshima and devised simply for the alliteration, we were told) was just one of the many family salutes given to the person of honor. Typically, everyone at the party sat in a circle, and all were asked to recount what they liked most about the birthday person—and such events weren't limited only to the kids. It was just as common to have the same scenario acted out for the adults when their birthdays rolled around. Don had a way of making everyone in his family—and his circle of friends—feel they were top priority with him and somehow, too, with the world in general.

He often said, "Every day should be exciting! Sometimes all you need to do is go for a walk in the woods, go for a ride, look at the stars, or just go and get an ice cream cone. Take people you love with you, or go by yourself." He, of course, usually took his family with him. "Just do *something* to make each day worth living—to create a memory you can call to mind when life gets you down."

Don made it a point every day, without fail, to visit his then 90-year-old mother, who lived nearby. He did his best to make her days exciting, as well, by bringing news of the family and taking her for short walks or rides in his convertible with the top down.

Don often said words that we, in turn, used over and over to ourselves and in raising our own family. He reiterated: "Joy doesn't come from things that cost money; it comes from discovering the world anew each day; it comes from seeing the world through the eyes of a child—sometimes acting like a child, if you need to, just to regain that sense of wonder. It comes, most of all, from truly loving those around you and receiving love from them in return. That's what real joy and happiness is all about."

Over the years, we wholeheartedly came to agree.

Long after we left California, a friend called to tell us Don had died. William Saroyan's words immediately came to mind: "A good man never dies ...". We felt this to be true, and we knew we really did not have to say "Goodbye" to a dear friend and exemplar—only "So long, Don ... and thanks."

THE SANTA CLAUS
PRINCI-"PAL"

He ran his school on the age-old premise of "The Golden Rule." It seemed simple enough, but this man would eventually have to suffer for the very simplicity of what he believed. However, I am ahead of myself in telling the story of a tremendously trying period in a dear friend's life as my family and I were to observe it.

Mr. Dunlap looked much like Santa Claus—minus the red suit and shiny black boots. With white hair, bushy white beard, a belly that would shake like jelly, and kindly blue eyes, he could have made a perfect department store candidate.

Tom and Dean hit it off immediately as co-principals within the huge San Juan School District of Northern California, one of the largest in the state. They were both jovial individuals, and neither were avid party-goers, so they paired off during the more lively administrative social get-togethers, where they shared funny stories and enjoyed each other's company.

Our sons, along with the vast majority of the parents and teachers in his school, adored "Mr. D". Kind and firm, yet friendly, he was a "hugger." He liked to hug the kids and hug the parents, and this, was at a time when such public physical gestures of affection were just beginning to come into question—especially in the schools.

Tom was of the Christian Scientist faith who believed deeply in its tenets. However, he was also deeply interested in the religious faiths of others, always asking penetrating questions about their beliefs, and giving those who believed differently than he did his utmost respect.

Tom loved children. He especially loved teaching them to sing. Each school year, at Christmas time and again in the spring, he would organize all the elementary grades into huge and popular children's choral productions. He taught the students all the great old songs such as Yankee Doodle Dandy, You're a Grand, Old Flag, Jeepers Creepers, and on, and on. He gave many who wanted to try out solo parts that built their self-esteem and generated much fun and many happy memories.

All five of our sons were fortunate enough to have Mr. Dunlap as their "Princi-PAL," as he jokingly referred to himself in person and on his letterhead.

Barry, our third, was just a tad reluctant to sing a solo, but "Mr. D" persuaded Barry to be the third member of a trio with two of his brothers, and what a fabulous job the three of them did with this first experience singing together. They dressed as three of the presidents for this number: Washington, Lincoln, and Carter as part of a spring program historical segment. What a delight the program was and how well received by everyone with plenty of laughter and applause.

Tom's hearty "Hellos" added a sparkle to every day. Nothing pleased Tom more than being a "Princi-PAL," and he did his best to live up to the title, all the while maintaining discipline and demanding respect in a way that other administrators often envied.

Since our home was only a block from Earl LeGette School, Tom would stop by now and then for a meal. He had recently been divorced, and we sensed his pain. We did what we could, as our busy schedule allowed, to try to help ease his burden. He often told us, "Whereas other friends say, 'Come for dinner sometime,' you two say, 'We're eating at five o'clock. Be there!'" He always seemed so appreciative of these gestures of friendship and later told us, "When I was going through my divorce, you saved my life by what you did for me."

At one meal together, I remember voicing a concern about the fact that our money never seemed to stretch quite far enough. In his wise and tender fashion, Tom said, "Nancy, have you ever been hungry? Have you ever not had a roof over your head?" In essence, I knew he was asking me, "Where's your faith?" He was a positive thinker, and I definitely needed the reminder that I did indeed have many blessings and that I needed to trust more in the God I believed in as sincerely as did our friend.

"You're absolutely right," I told him. "Thanks for the well-put prompt in the right direction." We both smiled.

Not long after, trouble, unexpectedly showed its face, and Tom wrenchingly had to endure the greatest ordeal of his life. Having moved to accept a principalship in another area of the district several miles from our home, it appeared he was having a difficult time with his new faculty. There was much in-fighting and jealousy, and a majority of the staff openly admitted they would have preferred a woman, then on the faculty, to Tom as principal.

The rancor simmered for some months, and finally a charge was brought against this always considerate person of "fondling," and other such nonsense. He was placed on probation and was not allowed to function as the school's principal in spite of years with a sterling record. The most devastating aspect of the bizarre situation was that he was never allowed to face his accusers. He, and we, and everyone who had known Tom well for years continually wondered how this could be happening.

Tom had a struggle not to fall into deep despair. Many friends and co-workers, including ourselves, held meetings and did our best to rally round him and give him support with our vocal and written votes of confidence. However, the school officials remained aloof and averse to allowing Tom to clear himself.

Weeks passed, and then the strangest of decisions put the roof on the crazily built structure of school district intrigue. Tom was offered the position of a sixth grade teacher in the San Juan District. He had often mentioned wanting to return to the classroom again but certainly not under these circumstances and as an obvious demotion.

The irony of the situation, obviously, was that if any of the related charges had been true, how could District officials place an alleged guilty person in a self-contained classroom, six hours every day in direct contact with young students and no other adults present? The idea seemed preposterous and untenable, but they did it nonetheless.

Many people believed the entire situation was a setup to remove Tom from the new principalship. If that was the case, the setup certainly worked.

However, to continue to meet his financial obligations, Tom took the position offered and finished off the last few years of his educational career in that job. We admired his courage in so doing, but often wondered how he was able to continue. We surmised that only his love for children and his love of teaching kept him working in that classroom—also perhaps the knowledge that he was at an age when finding other work would have been challenging at best.

Tom, had a family of several children with his first wife. As time went on, he met a lovely, understanding woman, also a teacher, who had several children of her own. The two had much in common, were married, and jumped into an exciting life of their own creation. They spent their summers volunteering as workers at a church camp and also at a Nevada dude ranch, as well as traveling to see their married children, and simply enjoying each other.

Thinking back, I have often reflected on the short-sightedness and sometimes downright evil that others can perpetrate on their fellow beings, and I realize this was no more in evidence than in Tom Dunlap's life. However, watching this gentle man cope with his pain strengthened every sensitive, caring person who knew him. This included Dean, myself, our sons, and hundreds of other students and parents who loved their "Princi-PAL" dearly.

When our boys were all grown, Tom would occasionally call the two of us to say "Hello" and ask "How are you doing?" He would query us individually about each of our sons, and would always share a bit of his wit and wisdom, along with a few laughs. We valued those calls through the years and forever considered the warmth of the friendship of our Santa Claus Princi-PAL a rare and special gift in our lives.

A FRIEND, A TRAGEDY

By her own admittance, she was a recluse.

I surmised, when we moved into the house next to hers, that she would probably not be the one to initiate a friendship. Later, I came to learn that she certainly did not like crowds of people. I also came to know that she allowed only a select few into her tiny circle of friends.

I liked the way she looked when I caught a glimpse of her from my kitchen window now and then, and I determined that before winter came on, I would at least make an overture of getting acquainted. Therefore, on a warm October day, as I spied her sweeping her driveway, I hurried over and said, "Hi, I'm your new neighbor."

Her quick smile brightened my day, as it would from that time on.

"I'm Mary Lou Tuffin," she volunteered. "Are you all moved in and settled?" Her voice sounded bright and intelligent.

"We're working on it," I replied. "It's been almost two months. It does take a while."

"Yes, I remember what it was like when my husband and I moved into this house almost twenty years ago," she said reflectively. "What do you and your husband do?"

I told her we were both involved at the university and that we were also free lance writers.

At that her ears perked up, and she said, "I did some editing in New York years ago. Before my husband died, he worked for McMillan Books, and we did some traveling associated with his job."

From that brief meeting on, our common interests made us friends.

Our age difference of 25 years melted into nothingness. We shared the interests of travel, books, writing, and music, and we both cared about people and their needs. There were differences, as well, but they faded quickly away. A heavy smoker, Mary Lou seemed remarkably healthy in spite of the long-time habit. I once told her, "I think you're in better shape than I am, Mary Lou"(though a deep, nagging cough spoke to a different reality). She quipped, "Maybe you ought to take up smoking," and we both chuckled.

A scientist, Mary Lou graduated with a degree in zoology. She was an avowed non-sentimentalist. Perhaps the two went together. She had no interest in religion or in life after death. She once shocked me by adamantly saying she would be disappointed if anything existed beyond this life. That statement was a particular surprise since she had revealed to me what a close relationship she and her husband, Dick, had shared. In my mind and heart, I felt she would desire the reassurance of seeing him again. Because of her love for this man, it only seemed natural to me that she would want to say, as Elizabeth Barrett Browning had said in one of her Sonnets to her beloved, Robert, "… if God choose, I shall but love thee better after death."

However, she remained adamant in her views, and I was only beginning to learn, through our relationship, just how different people can be and yet how close, in spite of those differences.

Though we did not share what I felt to be some of the deepest and richest spiritual and religious concepts of life, we nonetheless found much common ground, and I came to love this woman dearly.

She was thin yet did not appear frail. Her hearty personality revealed a tremendous solidness. Though in her late seventies when we met, her straight, bobbed hair was naturally black, her skin firm and amazingly free of wrinkles in spite of the dry Idaho weather. Perhaps this could be attributed to the earlier years of living in the East.

She often said her health and appearance were both inherited from her long-lived ancestors, mid-Westerners who had migrated to the small community of Vernal, Utah. Her father owned a photography shop there, and she grew up a non-Mormon in predominantly Mormon community. Her father collected many Indian artifacts of great value that were later donated to the local museum. Years after his death, it was Mary Lou's honor, along with her brother and sister, to attend the dedication of a wing of the city museum named in his behalf.

One winter Mary Lou and I attended a series of Beethoven piano concertos, the entire repertoire in fact, each performed once a month for eight months by Clive Swansborne, a British pianist and professor at Idaho State University. We felt privileged to hear the series and enjoyed so much sharing those hours together.

We took in a few movies now and again, but most of the time we sat in her living room listening to classical music or Dixieland Jazz, favorites of us both. More often, however, we would sit at her kitchen table and talk about an article she had read in **The Economist** or the **Wall Street Journal** or even the local **Idaho State Journal**. She took a particular interest in any writing Dean or I did, as well, and she became our "editor in residence." At this task, she was superb. She also did a considerable amount of typing for us but refused to accept pay for these jobs.

"I certainly do not need the money," she assured us, "and the jobs give me a sense of being useful," she would add.

As a small return for her help, we would take her to dinner now and again at Bei Jing, her favorite Oriental restaurant or out for a soup and sandwich lunch. She also seemed to enjoy my homemade soups, so every other week or so, I would take her whatever I had made. One year for Christmas Dean and I bought her a purple sweatshirt, part of her favorite attire (along with a pair of denim slacks). We ordered the shirt custom made with an embossed trophy cup and the words, "World's #1 Editor." That simple gift seemed to bring her special joy, and we noted that she wore the shirt often.

In our conversations, neither of us enjoyed the kind of chit-chat typical of some women, such as diets, cooking, what the neighbors were up to, and so forth. Both of us preferred other kinds of discussions—on books, politics, philosophy, and those reflecting deeper meanings of the human experience. That, of course, made our talks all the more interesting for both of us.

Mary Lou's greatest concern, and mine for her, was when she turned eighty and began to have trouble remembering. She would often say, "This poor brain of mine just isn't what it used to be."

In spite of this quickly developing set-back in her life, she continued to march on with a vibrant, lively outlook. Though it became more and more obvious that memory loss was definitely occurring, she utterly amazed me with her keen ability to read and understand and edit anything I would bring to her. Though she began to feel increasingly diminished, I considered her infinitely more bright and alive than most people half her age. However, the illness became worse and worse, and my concern for her grew, though there was little I could do except stand by and be a friend.

From Mary Lou I continued to learn just how different people can be and yet how similar—that far too many people close themselves off from others who do not believe as they do or because they may have habits or lifestyles different from their own. Perhaps it is simply a matter that most of us do not take the time to reach out and find that wonderful common ground that is almost always there—if we are willing to put forth the effort to discover it.

Mary Lou reached out with caring, not only to me but to Dean and our sons, and I often told the boys of the love Dean and I had for her. They also, I came to know, learned much from the friendship she and I shared. All of us were happy to know that Mary Lou financed a young Vietnamese student through his architectural degree. She was that kind of person.

I suppose it was her atheist/scientist stance that made her say, when a plane crashed with 300 people aboard, "Well, in a crowded world, that's 300 less mouths to feed." This always seemed so out of character to me.

As to our religious beliefs, I often wished I could have spoken candidly to her before she died. I would have said something like this: "Hats off to you, dear friend, for all you do. I love you dearly. Though it is one of those rather touchy subjects the two of us have avoided discussing at any length, I sincerely trust that you are wrong and I am right, at least in this one regard—that there *is* a life after death and that the two of us, with divine good fortune and good will, will share our very special friendship forever."

Mary Lou shot herself in her garage Sunday, October 20, 1997. I had visited with her just the day before, and we had chatted in her kitchen as we had done so many times before. Because of the violence of the act that she planned for and had chosen to commit, her loss became one of the deepest and most severe shocks of my life.

I still miss my friend; I always will.

A TIME FOR LEARNING
& GROWING

TEACHER

What is a teacher? In its simplest term, the word means "one who teaches; an instructor." Using that definition, it's obvious that almost all of us, in one way or another, are teachers every day of our lives. We set an example either good or bad; we show or help others; we share knowledge and insights; we often instruct others in doing something they previously did not know how to do or think in a way they had not thought before.

In considering our own teachers—and analyzing the best ones we have known—the question might be, "What makes a *good* teacher?"

As we think back over our lives, most of us can identify at least one or two individuals we would call great teachers who have impacted us in a positive way. However, it is often difficult to identify the qualities that make these people so important to us.

In my own life, I can point to several who have gone the "extra mile" and altered my life's course for the better:

First, my parents who were always there, always on the job, and therefore, always to be depended upon. Just an example or two illustrates their love and their ability to teach:

My father taught me a love of my ancestors just by talking often about them. I felt I knew my Grandmother Margaret because Dad told me what a good woman she was, how she worked as a governess before her marriage in the late 1800s, the sorrow she had of burying two little boys in Ireland before emigrating to America and then burying a five-year-old son after the family's move. He talked of her love of music and her devotion to her family.

Dad also told me incidents in the lives of my great-grandparents, how my great-grandfather, Samuel, worked in the shipyards of Glasgow, Scotland and died at age 30. Samuel's wife, Charlotte, had preceded him in death at age 24, leaving him with two small children to raise, one of them, my Grandfather William James McVeigh.

Another great-grandfather, William Killops, was a coachman on the beautiful Finnebrogue Estate near Bells Hill, County Down, North Ireland. William married Eliza White, and one of their children was my Grandmother Margaret.

These stories and so many more brought these people to life for me, and I have a reverence for those who were all a part of who I am, thanks to my father's teaching.

My mother, also, was an outstanding teacher who left me with many examples of wisdom that have benefitted me throughout my life. I remember one incident in particular. It occurred when, as a teenager, I was asked out on a date by a good looking boy who, unfortunately, had better manners at school than he did during the ending hours of our first date. I thought a lot of him and felt lucky to have been asked out by him. I was perhaps too proudly aware that I was the envy of several other girls at school. After the dance ended and we walked the dark road toward my home, I was totally surprised when my date began making some aggressive advances on my person. The details of the situation I would rather forget. Suffice it to say I resisted him and arrived home with a bright red face, tears in my eyes, and several ripped buttons on my clothes.

I totally expected my mother to say, "What on earth happened to you?" and to continue with similar logical and pressing questions until I revealed what had occurred.

Instead, in her remarkably wise way, she said nothing at all. She seemed to take in immediately what had probably transpired and determined that what I needed most was time to collect my emotions.

I hurried to the bath room, washed my face, changed my clothes and within a half hour I was ready to go back to the living room and tell her about it. Again, she said little, but I knew she understood my predicament. After a quiet hour, I went to bed, grateful for the time with her that had calmed and soothed my rumpled feathers as well as my aching teenage heart.

Both of these examples, and many more of my parents' teachings as I grew, served to remind me of what great people my parents were and of what great parental teaching is all about.

During my teenage years, another teacher that changed my life forever was my high school music teacher. His love, particularly for choir music, transferred itself into my being. It's hard to say exactly how; it just happened.

"Anything worth doing is worth doing well," was something he repeated over and over. "Music is a demanding mistress," he would say, and he, in turn, demanded everything his students could give.

Two of our sons had this same kind of music teacher in high school. His name was Dan Bowman, and his choirs of 120 students won all kinds of awards, as did his Gate City Singers, a select group of 24 who entertained at endless community events. He gave his all to his students, and they gave their all in return.

Yet one more remarkable teacher, among others I was fortunate to know, comes to mind. His name was Melvin Marion Gardner, but everyone called him "Bud". I was an adult when I met Bud, but he changed my life in a most remarkable way. It all began when I decided to sign up at a local community college in Sacramento, California, for a class called "Writing for Publication." I wrote about him in another vignette in this book called "Whence Cometh the Courage to Write?"

An ex-high school teacher and football coach, Bud was a handsome man, who would almost always be at the classroom door to greet each of his students with a handshake and a sincere smile. On the days when he ran a few minutes late, he would bound into the room, hurry to the front of the class, and then it was non-stop activity until the fifty minutes were at an end.

"Go for it!" he would say about a potential article. "I like this; I really like this!" he would add as he read through a piece. "Send it in; I can't imagine an editor refusing it!"

Such continual positive reinforcement gave many of us in the class impetus to overcome any hesitancy we might have about submitting a piece for publication. It gave us the desire and determination to succeed in seeing our work in print.

In his office, Bud kept a six-foot, highly-visible thermometer showing the money generated from the accumulated works of his students. The markings quickly soared into many thousands of dollars.

All the while, this highly motivating man never lost interest in his students. He had a keen memory for names and details, and he would touch base after the course was over and call and ask, "What's been happening? How are the sales going? Can I put in a good word for you with this editor or that? May I have a copy of your latest piece for my files?"

A great teacher? You bet.

Thinking back, I realize that *time* and *interest* and *caring* and *an urging toward achieving the best* seem to be the principal differences in great teachers and those we forget so quickly. Time given freely and unstintingly, plus unflagging interest shown in the welfare and needs of the "one," are all unselfish gifts given by great teachers, and all are key factors that change us, as individuals … enriching our lives and making us better people.

SOMETHING THERE IS ABOUT A CAMPUS

Robert Frost gave us the thought-provoking poem, Mending Wall, with the opening lines: "Something there is that doesn't love a wall." Taking off from this poem, I have had a parallel thought for years that often crosses my mind: "Something there is about a campus ... something that doesn't want to see learning ever end."

I have loved campuses all my life, from the day I entered kindergarten in Edgewood, Pennsylvania, a suburb of Pittsburgh to my high school days in Edinboro, to my early college days at Edinboro State University and beyond.

It was in high school that I began learning about Frost and other outstanding poets and artists—philosophers and historians—writers, and engineers, and scientists—and on and on.

It is on a campus where most of us really began to think about the world and our place in it. Not that marvelous learning cannot take place elsewhere. Nevertheless, it is on the campuses of the world where so much important learning takes place, where far-reaching careers and friendships begin, and where people can be lifted by dedicated teachers to a higher level of thinking and functioning than they otherwise might have achieved—particularly if they perceive and utilize the opportunities that are there for the taking.

Many high school campuses, it appears, seemed to have slipped greatly in their ability to inspire learning. Therefore, many of us must look to college and university campuses to carry on much of the learning and traditions that have been built on past millennia—back to the thinkers of the ages—Socrates, Plato, Aristotle, Hippocrates, Confucius, Emerson, Locke, and so many more.

Even when I'm not officially enrolled as a student on a campus, just walking through the grounds of an institution of higher learning is a kind of heartwarming experience. I love to gaze on the buildings, observe the students and teachers, take pleasure in the landscaping and foliage, listen to lectures, search in the libraries, attend plays, go to concerts, and more. I'm obviously one of those firm believers in life-long learning.

It has been my joy to have attended college classes for four decades now, beginning at Edinboro State University in Pennsylvania—a green and sprawling campus located in a small resort town south of Lake Erie. It was here that, as a 17-year-old freshman, I took entry-level biology, math, speech, English, and geography.

At the time, fresh out of high school (might that be where the term freshman originated?), I was terrified, especially of my speech class and its demanding and often harsh teacher, Mr. Vincent. On the other hand, Mr. Balliett, my English teacher, made me feel comfortable in class and somehow worthy.

He took the time to make comments on each paper and to discuss them at length, if clarification was needed. From him I developed a strong sense of talent as a writer. He affected my life deeply—and for the better.

What a difference one person can make in our lives—often, and particularly, in a campus-related setting.

Saying our "Hellos" in each campus classroom is always an interesting and rather intriguing experience—whether we are teachers or students (and I've had the fun of filling both roles). I've observed that almost everyone is a tad bit shy or reserved at first; then people gradually warm to each other, and when—at the end of each semester—we ultimately say our "Goodbyes," most of us seem to feel we were just getting acquainted. Much of the time the weeks fly by, and we are too soon on to other classes—each unit of learning, a door opened and often a welcoming portal to more learning as we enter (with the hope of not abandoning *all* hope, as the poet Dante warned).

After my marriage, I took numerous classes at several community colleges in California, as well as Sacramento State University. Dean willingly took care of our young boys so I could have this needed weekly break from the ongoing challenges of childcare.

Then, at age 50, after our sons were raised, and after pulling together all my credits, I finally finished my Bachelor's degree in Corporate Training at Idaho State University and ten years later my Master's degree in Human Resource Training and Development. I was not in a rush and simply loved taking classes, and learning, and growing.

In earlier years, while Dean earned his Doctorate on the lively campus of the University of California at Berkeley, we both enjoyed walking about the grounds there. Before that, we lived just a few blocks from the quieter campus of California State Polytechnic University at San Luis Obispo where Dean pursued his Master's degree.

On a much later trip to Canada, our family spent a couple of days at the University of Alberta in Edmonton where our son, as a visiting speaker, presented a workshop. There seemed to be huge trees everywhere on this campus and a vibrancy I found exhilarating—the same kind of vibrancy I had experienced when, as a teenager, my parents took me to see Yale, Harvard, and Princeton, those magnificent Eastern, Ivy League schools that are renowned throughout the world. I found it amazing how different each individual campus can be in its architecture and setting.

Later in life, I found this same kind of intriguing contrast when I had the great pleasure of visiting Oxford and Cambridge Universities in England. Both of these famous British schools have buildings that are still in use after nearly 1,000 years (and we often tear ours down in America after just a few decades).

Oxford University is comprised of many colleges located in various parts of the old town of Oxford, northwest of London, with its gorgeous Madeleine College. Cambridge, meanwhile, located northeast of the capital, is more centralized in the country, and I found it, overall, to be more dramatic in appearance. I was enthralled with the school's glorious Kings College, its expansive green lawns, its large and shady trees, and its stately buildings. To add to the charm are nearby gondolier-driven boats moving slowly under an arched bridge on the tranquil canal.

Well-known author C.S. Lewis lived and taught at Oxford; he also commuted to Cambridge to teach there as well. What a fortunate man to have spent his life in such a way—writing and teaching—both of which he loved so much—and on such impressive campuses.

At all these schools and many others, there is to me a distinct feeling of the upward reach of the human mind, a reaching that can, and should, and must lift mankind above the creatures of the lower kingdoms, if our species is to survive and if we are to avoid becoming animalistic ourselves.

At U.C. Berkeley, the Campanile bell tower rings out the hours, as clock towers do on many campuses. Just the compelling, pealing sound reminds all within hearing of the passing of time—and, one might hope, of the importance of doing something worthwhile with that precious commodity.

A wise and dear old lady once said, "No matter what age you are, always be taking a class when you possibly can; always be improving your mind." Over the years, I have found great satisfaction in taking her advice to heart. The classes I have taken have ranged from world literature, to marketing and management, to distance learning, psychology and philosophy, independent study classes, computer skills, and on, and on, and on. Those I still would like to take include geology, botany, zoology, advanced computer skills, all the literature classes I've missed, yoga, tai chi, and whatever else piques my interest.

I have learned much on the campuses where I have taken classes. I have, in turn, had the privilege of teaching at a university and, like C.S. Lewis, found joy, and satisfaction, and growth in so doing. Had I my wish, I would do this always—teach and learn, and teach and learn.

Something there is about a campus—rich, rewarding, sometimes puzzling, often overly-politicized, occasionally boring and mundane (depending on the individuals and subjects involved), but always the feeling that there is much more to be learned about the human condition and the human mind—its development and capabilities—than any of us ever begin to realize.

Something there is about a campus—a compelling and inspiring some- thing—a richness, an ongoing renewal, a beginning, an ending ... and a new beginning ... always a new beginning....

WHENCE COMETH THE COURAGE TO WRITE?

"Once more unto the breach, dear friends,
once more unto the breach ..."
Shakespeare's **Henry V**
3rd Act, 1st Scene

"Hi, this is Phil Osborne with *Reader's Digest*. We have your query on a story about laughter. We like the idea. Here's how we'd like to proceed...."

I hung up the phone, sat down, and took a deep breath. Dean and I? Write for **Reader's Digest**, the magazine with a monthly circulation of 27 million? This had to be one of the most hit-in-the-face-with-cold-water "Hellos" of my entire life.

Daunting? Inhibiting? A huge undertaking?

For a novice with this big-time publication, the challenge was all of the above. Could I do it? And from whence would come the courage and the ability?

From years past, I remembered lines from Shakespeare's **Henry V**: "Once more unto the breach, dear friends, once more unto the breach," and I suddenly realized I had faced the need for this same kind of courage—to break through my mind's resisting defenses—many times before.

Flashing into my memory came elementary school in a little college town in Northwestern Pennsylvania and Miss "Battleaxe" Barber, the small, gaunt-looking, black-haired teacher who could strike terror into the heart of any meek fourth grader.

I remember biting my fingernails till they bled the day she marched down the aisle, stopping just one desk ahead of mine to pull a shy, freckled-faced, red-headed farm boy, Ed Sanders, straight up out of his seat by his ear.... This for a small infraction.

Shortly after, she assigned an essay contest on dental health. (In retrospect, I think she should have been writing one about her own *mental* health.) Fourth graders writing essays? None of us knew where to begin. All I remember is the sense of dread and total inability I felt. However, fear can be the supreme motivator, so write the essay I did.

Next day, I was flabbergasted to hear Miss Barber's shrill voice announce my name as the winner. The prize? A toothbrush and tube of minty toothpaste.

By breaking through Shakespeare's "breach"—this time my own breach of terror—a love of word-smithing, or spinning words, became a budding and eventually a driving force in my life.

I remembered experiencing the same feeling of near panic the afternoon I was assigned my final theme in a Freshman English class at Edinboro State University, also in Northwestern Pennsylvania. It was fall, and I chose the weighty title: "Autumn and Death are Synonymous." Everyone in the class knew the professor was a tough grader, and I had given my all to every writing effort put forth for him that semester. This last assignment, however, was a big part of our final grade, so my apprehensions were running high.

In spite of the sense of ineptitude I felt, the theme seemed to flow. I couldn't wait for it to be returned, and when it finally was, I turned mine over to see the coveted "A" followed by a powerfully hand-written note from this teacher I had come to admire. After the grade he scrawled: "I hope you continue to read and write ... and read and write ... and read and write...."

That courage to write, followed by the exhilarating feeling of breaking through, was mine once again.

Time passed, and with marriage, five sons born close, and a husband in graduate work at the University of California, Berkeley, there was little time to pursue my love of writing. However, as the two of us watched the strain of the doctoral program break marriages apart in our huge married student housing complex, we decided to make his degree a united effort. My part in the process was helping polish his many papers and later editing and typing his 300-page dissertation—*pre* word processing days. Though we didn't realize it at the time, this was the beginning of our many adventures as a collaborative writing team.

Following our exciting days at Berkeley, we moved to Sacramento where I dabbled at writing, as time allowed. It was there that, despite the pressures of our growing brood of sons, I signed up for Bud Gardner's popular "Writing for Publication" course at Sacramento State University mentioned previously.

Defining moment in my writing life? This had to be it.

It was Bud who gave me the courage to go ***unto the breach*** time and time again. He seemed bent on motiving every student to conquer their fears and "submit, submit, submit those articles," as he would say. It was almost like Winston Churchill saying, "Never give in. Never, never, never ..."

On my very first submission, he boldly wrote, "THIS IS GREAT! GO FOR IT! SEND IT TODAY!"

Because of his remarkable ability as a teacher and mentor, I boldly fired off that short article he thought was so great to **Good Housekeeping**. Shortly after, the phone rang and a voice from New York City said, "We like your piece. Will you take $1000?"

Bud always tells his students, when they receive such a call, to say, "Is that all?"

However, I forgot the counsel and simply stammered, "Sure."

With only a few minor changes, my first solo, nationally distributed magazine article was in print, and joy was mine.

This was the beginning of many more such writing experiences. Each involved a risk. Many articles were rejected. Few have garnered large sums of money. However, the beckoning finger of the sorceress of words is always there: **Write, write, write**.

So ... with these experiences and other positive writing moments to look back on, I felt I was ready to take on *Reader's Digest*. Writing collaboratively with my ever-encouraging husband, we broke down any inhibitions—mine more than Dean's—and worked enthusiastically with our editor, Phil Osborne.

Six months later, with two fact finding field trips from our new home in Idaho to sunny California (paid for by the *Digest*) and what seemed like endless research behind us, our article "Take Time to Laugh" appeared on the newsstands in the largest circulated magazine in the world.

Victory!

Now, five published books and many hundreds of published articles later, I still find that each writing challenge involves the act of going **unto the breach** and breaking through.

I often wonder what gives writers the courage to launch their wits against the inevitable blank piece of paper or vacant computer screen? Of course, it's simply the fact that each of us has gone **unto the breach** time and time again in our lives, and we know in our hearts we can go unto it once again.

LESSONS LEARNED FROM LAWN MOWING

Me? Mow a lawn? Never!

Why should I, I often thought to myself. I have several sons and a hunk of a husband? Mowing and yard work was their bailiwick, and it simply never crossed my mind to even want to try it. I simply figured they would do that job ... and so they did for many years.

Then the inevitable occurred. The sons got married, and the husband had to be gone a lot, so one day I pried myself away from my computer and took a wary look at our scruffy, overgrown lawn. Then I ventured into the garage and took a somewhat hesitant look at our big, red and black gas mower. Lastly, I said to myself, "I think I just may attempt the impossible."

And guess what? Mowing our lawn that day turned out to be more than I bargained for in many ways. In fact, as I continued to mow each week, I learned several revealing things that wonderful summer.

Instead of a "summer of discontent," this became for me a summer of great content. It even became an epiphany, of sorts. Strangely, just by pushing a humming machine over blades of fast-growing, errant grass, I awakened to a whole new realization of who I was, and I learned several revelations about life and about myself. For example:

• This kind of work was a whole new domain for me. It became one that I tackled with gusto and accomplished with pride. I found I could do something I never, ever thought I could or would do. *When we overcome any obstacle in our lives, we gain a new kind of confidence in other areas as well*.

• Once I got started on my weekly routine, I found I looked forward to the task. I almost hoped the grass would grow a little faster so I could have the same satisfaction I had the first time I mowed. Here was a task that virtually asked to be done; it was manageable—it had a defined beginning and end; it didn't take more than an hour to do, and I could bask in the golf-course-like look of the finished product. ***Satisfaction often comes to us in unexpected ways.***

• Mowing is somewhat akin to learning to drive a car. Just as when I turned the key in my car's ignition for the first time, so I was equally unfamiliar with the mower's starting mechanism. The thing took off, and I was not in immediate control. My initial rows were less than straight, and I bumped into a couple of trees and broke a ceramic lawn ornament. However, I learned quickly how to manage the machine, and little by little I found myself refining my abilities. As a wise person once said, ***"That which we persist in doing becomes easier to do, not that the nature of the thing has changed, but that our ability to do has increased."***

• Some days I did not (and still do not) have the muscle power to get our old mower started, so I have to ask for help. Relying on others is part of living, of course. ***Much as we might like to, we simply cannot do everything we want to do by ourselves.***

• As with many tasks, one thing leads to another, and after mowing, I next found myself wanting to make the lawn even more attractive, so I decided to pull a pail of dandelions every other day or so. Gardening can be a humbling experience. We have to get on our knees to work in the soil. I found myself relaxing, while at the same time using new muscles and feeling a release of stress. ***All of us can find new ways to let off steam, get some needed exercise, and, yes, be a little more humble in the process.***

• Another wise person once said, "Survey wide fields; cultivate small ones." This, too, was a lesson I learned. Only so much can be done each day, and it's wise to plot out what we feel will accomplish the most good in the least amount of time. ***We can learn not to attempt too much but to school ourselves in setting priorities, sticking to them, and being satisfied with a small sense of accomplishment each day.***

• Weeds, I have rapidly learned, are like bad habits. Yank them out while they are small, or they will proliferate to unmanageable proportions. Just as it's wise to be on the "lawn alert" and eradicate pesky weeds when they first present themselves, so it is equally wise to be vigilant in improving ourselves. ***We are smart*** *when we quickly and purposely eliminate those things that detract from our personal progress.*

• Working with plants at various seasons has reminded me of the ongoing nature of life. Just as spring presents itself to us in all its glory, followed by the warmth of summer, the chill of fall, and the cold of winter, so our lives move on in their inevitable cycles. *It's wise to realize that life on earth is temporary and to choose the best ways to use the time allotted to us.*

• My morning hour spent in the yard has become a welcome routine. I have ventured further than the mowing and the weeding and have even begun sawing dead tree limbs and clipping hedges. *More and more tasks present themselves in our lives, and we can enjoy the variety and sense of accomplishment in all of them.*

• Flowers are the next item on my list of attempts at beautification. I am currently buying books on correct trimming and on ornamental horticulture. I have even determined to take a class or two to enhance my skills in several areas of this rewarding outdoor work. *We can always be expanding our hearts and minds.*

Can this really be me, I sometimes ask myself? The bookworm, the writer, the "inside-the-house person" who never had a desire to get my hands in the dirt?

Incidentally, I did buy a good pair of garden gloves which have saved the fingernails, and no one is the wiser about my early morning activities. I don't really care, of course, if my work is known. In fact, I often find occasion to share my new-found hobby with others.

Some people have already noticed. My next door neighbor stopped by one day as I was running the weed-eater and said, "You're getting pretty good at that stuff!" I considered this a compliment from a man who works hard to keep his own place looking attractive.

Bill, another neighbor, does a little yard work almost every day. I notice his wife remains indoors. (She doesn't know what she is missing.) Over the fence, he and I often chat about lawn and garden interests. One day I learned that we also share a great interest in books. He recently loaned me a favorite of his, and through both interests we have become good friends—all because I was out mowing my lawn and pulling weeds. There's a camaraderie among the lawn-mowing set, I've found.

Well, I could talk more on the adventures of that delightful summer that changed my outlook on life so much, but I think the idea is obvious.

P.S. If you haven't attempted mowing the lawn or some other such activity, you might just want to give it a try.

THE OLD MAN BY THE SIDE OF THE ROAD

When a person or family moves and says "Hello" to a new neighborhood or a new community, a good attitude about that move is of inestimable importance, and we can all learn much from this kind of experience.

While at an appointment with a new, young dermatologist in our town, he immediately said, as he entered the examining room, "I know your family. About ten years ago, you and your husband spoke at a church meeting for young people that I attended. Your husband told a story that has had a major impact on my life. Since I married, my family and I have moved many times because of my schooling, and that story has made those moves much more pleasant than they otherwise might have been."

I said, "Really? I don't remember; what story was it?"

I was surprised when he continued, "You're my last patient of the day, so I'll take a little time to recall that wonderful, little story. It was about an old man sitting by the side of the road as a car approached with a family inside.

"The father stopped the car, asked his wife to roll down the window, and he said to the old man, 'Hi. We're moving into your town up ahead. You look like you might be from around here. What kind of town is it anyway'?

"The old man replied, 'What kind of town are you coming from?'

"The father said, "Oh, it was a lousy place; that's why we're moving. The people were rude, the local officials were all corrupt. The schools were rotten. We couldn't wait to get out of there."

"The old man replied, 'Well, sorry you had to make the move, 'cause that's exactly the same way this town is. So you probably wasted your time coming here.'

"Later that same day, another car with another family passed by the old man. The father in the vehicle backed up the car, asked his wife to roll down the window and then asked the old man essentially the same question: "We're moving here today. What kind of town is this anyway?'

"The old man replied, 'What kind of town are you moving from?'

"And the father said, 'We really hated to leave; it was a wonderful town. The people were friendly and kind, the local government did a pretty good job most of the time. Our kids did great in school and had lots of friends.'

"To which the old man replied, 'That's exactly the way this town is. I think you're going to be very happy here.'"

I had recognized the story right away, but I enjoyed the young doctor's retelling of it.

We both agreed that this little allegory, of course, only points up what has been written and said about the importance of attitude. This important mind-set can be so beneficial in all the many circumstances of our lives—in school, at work, at home.

Attitude is *altitude*, some have said.

Essentially, attitude is *everything*.

THE BOY WHO COULD SLEEP WHEN THE WIND BLOWS

Stories often have a profound effect on all of us as we learn and grow. The beginning and the ending are critical, of course, to a good tale—a kind of "Saying Hello" and "Waving Goodbye."

Take notice when a speaker goes from the generalities of a talk into a story. If it's any kind of a story at all, eyes rivet, fidgeting reduces to a minimum, and the audience is "with the speaker" until the tale is told.

Since time immemorial, the best of stories have not only a beginning and an ending but also a moral—a lesson that can be applied in one's own life.

So it was with a story a speaker told many years ago. Now, when I prepare well ahead for a trip, when I do an assignment long before it's due, when I consider eventualities and prepare for them in advance of the circumstances, I am reminded of this remarkable, yet not-so-well-known tale.

◆   ◆   ◆

A farmer needed to hire some help for the summer, so he posted a "HELP WANTED" sign by his farm gate.

Several young men stopped to apply, and the farmer asked each one his name and qualifications. One boy said, without much enthusiasm, "Oh, I'm Jim, and I've worked on a couple of farms now 'n then."

Another said, "My name's Tom. I ain't done much farmin', but I done other kinds a work. Right now I just need a job so's I can get some extra cash."

Neither of the boys, nor several others who stopped by, impressed the farmer. They all lacked the vitality he was looking for, and he thought to himself, "I'd as soon do the work myself as hire a boy that has no spunk about him."

Just as he was about to take down his sign, he noticed a young man with his shoulders back and his head held high walking swiftly down the road. He waved to the farmer and said, "I heard in town that you're lookin' for some hired help for the summer."

As he had done with the other boys, the farmer said, "Tell me your name, young man, and your qualifications for the job."

With a twinkle in his eye and a smile on his face the youth said, "Well, sir, my name's Joe, and as for qualifications, I can sleep when the wind blows."

The farmer scratched his head. He thought he had heard everything, but this was something he certainly had not heard before. He was intrigued by the look of the young man. Curious about him, he decided to hire him on the spot without questioning him about what he meant by being able to sleep when the wind blows.

The farmer removed his sign and said, "You've got yourself a job, Joe. You can wash up behind the house, and you can sleep in the barn loft. There's blankets and a pillow in the tack room. My wife Martha'll bring you some dinner at suppertime. We start in the fields at sunup."

"I like the looks of him," he later told his wife. "He's got some muscle, Martha, and unless I miss my guess, he's an honest young man who can do a day's work."

With this brief introduction to the couple, Joe began his work at the farm. Each day he did as the farmer asked, and the two of them quickly fell into the routine of the summer tasks. The farmer was grateful to have the extra help, and the boy was happy to be earning his way.

One evening after the three were asleep, an unexpected summer storm hit the area. The wind and lightning were fierce. At one terrific clap of thunder the farmer and his wife wakened. Both of them realized immediately that this storm was gale force in intensity.

Quickly the farmer yelled to his wife as he grabbed for his trousers and shoes, "Martha, this here's a bad one. I didn't batten things down for a hum-dinger like this. I gotta get Joe before we lose the stock and everything blows away."

Running to the barn loft, the farmer yelled, "Joe! Joe!"

In spite of the tempest force winds, the farmer found Joe sleeping soundly in the loft. Perplexed, he shook the farm-hand's shoulder and cried, "Joe, wake up, we gotta hurry. The wind's gonna blow the farm to kingdom come!"

Sleepily Joe opened his eyes and said, "Mr. Jones, didn't I tell ya when I hired on that I can sleep when the wind blows?"

"Sure you did, but...."

"Well, just go on back to bed then, and rest easy. I secured the stock and tied everything down on the place that could be tied down. I been doin' that every night since I got here. That's what I meant when I told ya I could sleep when the wind blows."

"You did?" queried the farmer.

"Sure. My pa always taught me to consider in my mind about anything that might come to pass, then prepare for it ahead o' time. That ways, he always told me, I wouldn't have any trouble sleeping when the wind blows."

The farmer could hardly believe his ears. He left Joe and hurried back to the house. On the way he checked all the gates and found every item on the farm tethered securely against any amount of wind other than a true tornado.

"By cracky," he said to his wife, as he entered the house. "That young feller was way ahead o' me. He didn't assume like I did that there wouldn't be a storm comin'. He just prepared ahead in case one might hit."

He was still muttering to himself, as he crawled back into bed.

Long after Joe left the farm, the farmer reflected on the important lesson he had learned from his farmhand, Joe—the boy who could sleep when the wind blows."

LEARNING FROM OUR LITTLE ONES

Our oldest son, Glenn, was born in the springtime of the year. When we beheld that tiny boy, our joy was more full than it had ever been. We learn so much from our first child.

As this new wonder in our lives grew from a baby into a darling little boy, we appreciated the exceptionally kind and gentle nature of our first-born son. From an early age Glenn loved to read and was so eager to learn. I remember holding his hand when he was three and walking by some flowers. He wanted to stop and smell their sweetness, and we both delighted in their beauty.

Then, on another rainy day in Oakland, California, Dean and I each took one of his little hands in ours and ran with him through the cool summer rain, giggling and having the time of our lives as the wind blew us along. Glenn was wearing his little yellow raincoat, and we three probably looked like a scene out of *Curious George*, minus the monkey.

Now that Glenn is grown and married, the memories remain sweet of our first little boy and the joy we had of learning to appreciate so many things more fully because of him.

Most of all Glenn, as he grew, taught our family new dimensions in unselfish leadership. He was four years old when his next younger brother, Matthew, was born.

Glenn, with his unmistakable leadership qualities, led out at an early age with his brothers and often actually helped us, in many ways, parent them. When Matthew arrived, Glenn willingly took on some of the feeding and changing of his younger brother, and as the two of them grew, they became great friends.

"I like being a big brother," Glenn would say. "I'm good at helping," he would add over and over and, we, of course, were delighted. Sometimes we felt we were even taking advantage of his willingness to be such a "super older bro," as he later called himself.

A year and a half after Matthew was born, Barry joined the family, and then Robert and Gregory came along in quick succession. As each of his younger brothers grew and had their birthday parties, Glenn pitched in, organized the games, and helped supervise most of the activities. He did this in such a willing way that I often simply watched, and admired, and wished I had more of these special talents myself.

Now the father of five children himself, we continue to observe Glenn, along with his good wife, Debbie, doing his best to raise his own young family in a difficult world.

Matthew, our February child gave us, among other lessons, the important one of perseverance. This quiet, loving son was born with mild cerebral palsy. We often felt gratitude that his case was not as severe as many others, and from Matthew we learned what it is to cope with a physical challenge.

Throughout his life Matthew has had to struggle a bit harder than the average person to achieve. For us, he has exemplified the proverbial tortoise, who beat the hare, teaching us much about the race of life.

Barry, meanwhile, made his entrance just a week before Christmas—a very special gift to us at a special time of year.

Barry is one who often smooths the way for others. He has the talent of being able to fix almost anything—cars, household items, and on, and on—the only one in the family so blessed. He is also the family artist and has used his talent to create many lovely pieces of stained glass, paintings, etchings, and so much more. He is often painstaking in his work, desiring to be as perfect as he can.

He became diabetic at age seven and therefore had to deal with greater highs and lows than the rest of us in the family, but he keeps coping and keeps trying. He has a laugh that is a delight to share, and we admire him for the unique lessons in living he provides for us.

Robert, our only summer child, came to us in the heat of July. We sometimes called him our "hot sketch," an old New England term for a rowdy, little imp.

Robbie (and later Robb), as we nick-named him, was the one who simply seemed to never give up. He was the major musician of the family. From an early age, he exhibited a talent for the piano. As a teenager, he would practice endless hours—many times months—for a competition and then lose to someone else. Never evidencing discouragement, he would say, "I'll go for it again." And so he did until he finally won the privilege of playing a concerto with the local symphony orchestra. There were many "Bravos" from the audience. Again, to us as parents, this was a lesson in living, and one we benefitted from observing.

When Robb was seven months old, we learned we were expecting our last child and we began to wonder how we could handle another baby so close. However, with enough faith, strength comes from somewhere to cope with whatever challenges we face. As he grew, Greg's four older brothers and, we too, enjoyed him so much. We all continue to do so.

On one of Aunt Mary and Uncle Ken's annual visits, Glenn and Matthew showed off their sports and Scouting achievements, Barry proudly displayed his latest art creation, Robb played some tunes on the piano, and Aunt Mary said to three-year-old Greg, "And what do you do?" He thought for a minute and then proudly said, "I smile a lot." And with that he grinned from ear to ear.

As it turned out, there were many other talents in the youngest member of the family—not only his beautiful singing voice but his ability to be an example for the rest of us in taking every opportunity to see a need and fill that need. He serves others unselfishly, and willingly, and well.

This is not to say any of the various qualities we have mentioned are unique to any of the boys. It is not to say, either, that any of them are perfect. It is to say that, we, as parents have learned from all of them, and we are so grateful for what we have learned.

Family life surely has to be the greatest school of all. It is from our children that we can learn much of what our sojourn on the earth really means to us and how we can try to live life to its fullest.

LIFE FLIGHT LEGACY

While sleeping soundly, the telephone's insistent ringing at five a.m. jarred us from a final hour of rest. On the other end of the line, the voice of our daughter-in-law carried with it that concerned sound we had heard many times before. "We're heading to the ER," she said. "We're afraid there's a problem with Barry's transplant."

"We'll meet you there," was all my husband said.

Both of us dressed quickly and hurried to the medical center near our home in Southeast Idaho to find our 34-year-old son, Barry, and his wife Brenda in one of the curtained examining rooms. The typical acrid smells filled the air. Barry, pale and lying on the bed, said nothing as we entered. He just looked at us, and I sensed the pleading in his eyes.

Our eyes, in turn, went to the young physician bending over our son.

"It may be appendicitis," he said. "We're just not sure."

X-rays were ordered, and the four of us waited anxiously for results, Barry stoically enduring the pain that showed all too clearly on his face. His strong, muscular body belied the years of internal ravaging that the disease of diabetes had inflicted on him.

"I don't want to go back there," he said, deep concern punctuating every word.

"Back there" meant the University of Minnesota Transplant Center in Minneapolis.

We understood his fears, all the while realizing the choice would not lie with Barry nor with those of us who could only stand at his side and watch, and wait, and pray.

The pain continued unabated, and the ER doctor concurred with Barry's surgeon by phone at UMN that our son needed to be rushed to the place where his second pancreas transplant had occurred just 90 days earlier. No one knew for sure what was going wrong, and the fear of rejection was in everyone's minds.

"Get him here as fast as you can," came the word, but hours passed before the small Lear jet could be flown from Boise, Idaho's State Capital, to our tiny Pocatello airport.

Jan Simmons, the life-flight nurse standing outside the examining room, advised us almost tersely, "There's only space in the plane for Barry and two other family members; even then, it'll be tight," she said.

Dean looked into my eyes, and I into his. The years of dealing with our son's disease had been trying for both of us, but we had hung together through it all, doing our best to understand each other's needs as well as those of our son. Without words, we understood immediately, however, that Brenda needed to be with Barry and that only one of us would be able to accompany the two of them on the life flight. I assumed Dean should go, but he instinctively knew how much I wanted to be with Barry.

"I want you to go; I'll catch the first Delta flight in the morning," he said, and my heart filled hearing those unselfish words.

Delta Airlines, it must be noted, had been a godsend to us during the entire previous year. Once a donor was found, Barry had to be in Minneapolis within hours. Of all the airlines we had contacted for our emergency transportation needs, it was Delta's Community Affairs Department that responded quickly and efficiently, thus making Barry's emergency trips to Minnesota a possibility for our family. We will be forever grateful for all they did.

This trip, however, became a Lear jet life flight and Delta would not be involved.

The tense hour before the flight was incredibly rushed as Brenda and I dashed to our homes for necessities. Dean and I then followed behind the ambulance that was carrying Barry and Brenda to our community airport. On the tarmac sat the sleek little plane that was to make the flight to Minneapolis at a cost of $27,000. Fortunately, Barry's insurance would cover this cost and the majority of his transplant costs as well. Our gratitude for this blessing in our lives was overwhelming, and we were grateful, at the time, to be able to pay the costs not covered for our son.

The owner and pilot of the aircraft came into the Av Center and was quick to learn that Dean and I had both hoped to go with our son but realized we could not. He surprised us by saying, "No problem; I don't have a copilot with me on this one, and one of you can take a seat up front with me."

Dean and I looked at each other.

"I didn't even bring a toothbrush," Dean said.

"Go with us; we can buy what you need there," I begged. "We all need you."

And so the decision was made.

Within minutes, Dean and the pilot were in the cockpit, and the gurney carrying our son was wheeled from the ambulance. He was lifted by several medical personnel into the small, cylindrical jet.

I sat toward the front of the plane, my seat facing the rear. Brenda sat across from me, also facing the same direction. Jim Jensen, the accompanying EMT, occupied a seat between the two of us and the cockpit, and Barry, lying on his narrow bed, was at the rear of the plane just a few feet away facing the rest of us, along with his nurse, Jan Simmons, seated by his head. The total space in the plane seemed only about 20' x 5', and I felt as though I were in a miniature submarine. The roar of the engines filled the chilly air at takeoff; then Jan carefully monitored Barry's IV and his vitals and continued to do so throughout the three-hour flight.

As I looked into the face of my son, thoughts of all that had transpired the past several years passed quickly through my mind. Gazing at his strikingly handsome young face, I couldn't help but notice that his dark brown hair and even darker eyebrows and eyelashes appeared even more dark against the stark white pillow, outlining the extreme blueness of his eyes.

During the intense experience of this life flight, I was to learn much about my son and about myself. The experience was to leave with me a legacy that would forever change my way of thinking about life and about those I love so much.

My thoughts went to the January day 26 years earlier when I walked with Barry's hand in mine into the Kaiser Permanente Medical Center in Sacramento, California. He was only six years old when we learned he had the most severe form of diabetes.

All through his growing up years, we and Barry both had to make the adjustments to living with this insidious disease. This was not easy, especially during his teenage years when he was the only diabetic youth in his school. However, he persevered, and life went on for Barry and his two older and two younger siblings—five brothers who all developed a special bond one with another that has remained firm through the years.

At 21, Barry married Brenda Knight, a sweet girl who presented him with two beautiful children, first our demure and darling Jenny and four years later, little red-headed, freckle-faced Austin. During these years, the complications of Barry's disease grew worse, mainly because of hypoglycemic unawareness, the life-threatening inability to sense his low blood sugar levels. Even with walking the tightrope of diet, exercise, multiple daily testing, and insulin injections, he could rapidly drop, uncontrollably, into a semi or totally unconscious state.

For the better part of ten years, Brenda would call at all times of the day and night, and Dean would go speeding across town to help. Other times, the low blood sugars were so severe that the EMT's were summoned—often in the middle of the night, to rapidly administer IVs—providing Barry with the glucose needed to prevent brain damage and return him to consciousness. Convulsions could sometimes occur during these episodes, and these were frightening to witness. Later Barry's eyes and other parts of his body also began to exhibit the damage often inherent from years of living with diabetes.

Then, after much research on our options and a work-up at the Diabetes Research Center in Miami, circumstances led us to the University of Minnesota, one of the premier pancreas transplant centers in the nation.

"Barry, we feel strongly that a full pancreas transplant will be your best chance for a normal life. It's best to consider it now while you have the health and strength to withstand the operation." This was the word from the chief examining physician and his associates.

"It's best to do it now before you begin to experience any further complications or chance of dying in an auto accident."

Along with the conclusions of these surgeons, Barry and Brenda made the difficult decision to go ahead. Once on the transplant list, Barry had several false calls. Finally a matching donor was found, and Delta (always holding two seats for Barry and Brenda on every flight from our closest major airport in Salt Lake City without the need for advance purchase requirements) flew them both to Minnesota for his transplant on September 22, 2000.

For three wonderful days, our son was insulin-free; then the unthinkable happened. The transplant failed due to a blood clot. Prior to the surgery, Dean and I had put our two dear ones on the plane, then followed quickly by car to Minnesota. The day after we arrived, Barry developed the horrible pain of thrombosis, and with no new donor organ available to replace the failed one, Barry was operated on again and the transplanted organ removed.

When the news first hit, the sadness and disappointment we all felt was incredible. However, as Barry began to recover, he comforted us by saying simply, "I'll be okay," even though we knew he felt the tremendous loss more than any of us. I stroked his hair, and the four of us hugged each other—all of us needing the help of heartfelt love that day.

This son of ours, strong of body, returned quickly to his customary look of a buffed football player, belying his illness. He also returned to the demands and the continuing complications of long-term, insulin-dependent diabetes.

Three months later on the afternoon of New Year's Eve, another call came from UMN, this time from the well-known and highly respected chief transplant surgeon, Dr. David Sutherland.

"We have a wonderful matching organ," he said, "I think Barry should take it."

"Can we—should we—go through this again?" The question hung in all our hearts, certainly most especially for Barry.

Once more the rush to the airport in Salt Lake City for the reserved Delta seating space, this time through cold and foggy weather resulting in a delayed—almost postponed—takeoff for Barry and Brenda.

Back in Minneapolis once more, the normal eight-hour surgery—because of excessive scar tissue from Barry's previous transplant—turned into thirteen grueling hours. Our son nearly died on the operating table. Dean and I, meanwhile, hung anxiously by the phone waiting for Brenda's call.

"It looks good," she said when it was finally over. "An artery was cut, and he needed nine units of blood. Dr. Sutherland said it was the most difficult transplant he had done in twenty years, but it looks good. The recovery time will be longer, but everything points to success this time."

We, meanwhile, helped at home by caring for Jenny and Austin for a week, constantly staying in touch for news of the recovery. Then, as before, we left our two grandchildren with their other set of grandparents and drove the 1,000 miles to be with our son and his wife during the final days at the hospital, and later taking him and Brenda to the airport for their return flight home. There he recovered once again, this time more slowly but all the while able to live his life without insulin shots and without the terrible low blood sugar episodes.

Now, three months had passed since the second transplant and this night in the tiny airplane.

My reverie came to an end on the jetted life flight, as I looked at Barry enduring yet more pain. I wondered how another trip to Minnesota could be happening. Why? If another surgery was needed, how much could even Barry's strong body endure? He had been opened in September, then three days later opened again to remove the failed transplant. The second, successful transplant had required a return to surgery a day later for a washout of the blood that had accumulated in his abdomen. Now a fifth opening of his body threatened.

My mother's heart went out to my son, as I am certain all mothers' hearts go out to their children who suffer—many until the final "Goodbye" of mortality is said. My dear grandmother, who lost a daughter when the girl was 23, often said that this loss was the hardest one of all to bear—that of the death of a child.

I realized, through my own pain, and through all the tears and prayers of all the years of Barry's illness, that there is no real and satisfying answer—at least not in this earthly realm it would seem—to that immense and ever-nagging question: "*Why?*"

Yes, there are the same kinds of philosophical answers posed by Job's friends that have filled the millennia, there are the many religious postulates, many of which make sense in their own right. However, when it is you or your loved ones who must endure suffering in its most virulent forms, none of these seemingly pat answers seems to assuage the grief and pain.

My own comfort, however, suddenly came on that life flight to Minneapolis as I stared longingly at my son, trying hard not to show my worry and concern. It came quietly to my mind in words I had memorized as a child from the Proverbs of Solomon—words that have reverberated through the centuries: "Trust in the Lord with all thine heart and lean not to thine own understanding."

Somehow, taking counsel from those words, and knowing Dean's remarkable strength as husband and father and my own inner strength as wife and mother, I realized that somehow, someway we would be sustained and be able to go forward with faith, no matter what—and no matter how hard the road ahead might be for all of us.

I came, also, to appreciate just how deeply I loved this wonderful son of ours, how precious he was to me. This blinding revelation was also a part of this life flight legacy. I had loved Barry since the day of his birth. I had loved him as a child, remembering so well the day he was diagnosed with diabetes and the day Dean and I left him with aching hearts as an eight-year-old at a diabetic camp for children in California's beautiful Kings Canyon National Forest—a place where he could spend time with other children coping with their vital and essential daily insulin regimens.

I had loved him through the difficult teenage years, as he struggled with the never-ending demands of his disease and on through the rigors of his transition into manhood. All the previous years, since we welcomed him into the world, had been filled with challenges, yet I realized that I loved Barry even more now, as I watched him deal in his own way with this latest adversity—that of looking once again into the starkness of his own mortality at far too young an age.

The life flight came to an end on the chilly evening of March 31 as bright stars sparkled brilliantly overhead. We looked down on the city lights of Minneapolis, gleaming like millions of glittering jewels on the velvety black earth below. Even with pain and suffering so much with us that night, the glories of our earth—and our lives on it—brought vividly to my mind the fact that there is much more meaning to this life—and to our very reason for being—than most of us take the time in our busy lives to deeply ponder. It was all such a great lesson learned in those tense and stressful hours as the airplane engines drowned out all other sound.

A waiting ambulance rushed Barry and Brenda to the hospital. Dean and I followed by taxi, seeing billboards flash by and talking absent-mindedly with our driver about the need for our rush to the University Transplant Center.

Once again, in those all too familiar surroundings, Barry's physicians pondered the cause of the pain. The black spot on the x-ray seemed to offer no clue as to what the actual problem might be.

Though we had all prayed it might be otherwise, the decision came quickly:

"We have to go in and see what's going on," his surgeon said. "There's just no other choice."

Each of us, including the doctors, understood the life-threatening nature of another surgery, but those of us closest to Barry—and Barry himself—all tried to remain strong for each other and for our own sanity. I held back the overwhelming need to cry until after Barry looked pleadingly into our eyes and was rolled away to the operating room.

Prior to going, he asked Brenda to tell their little ones how much he loved them.

Four hours later, after walking the quiet halls and waiting and praying, the surgeon came into the room and said, "It's good we took him when we did. There was a narrowing of the duodenal lining and had it burst, it's unlikely we could have saved him. However, we repaired the problem. We also re-routed his bowel around the new pancreas. It looks like he's going to be okay."

Relieved, we still had to face yet even more questions dealing with "Why?" These questions again begged answering, as the complications of Barry's surgeries left him with two years of extreme suffering caused by the severing of a major nerve leading from his spine into his right leg. The long-term administration of narcotics never completely masked the insidious, unrelenting pain.

This complication was followed by the shriveling of the big muscle in the calf of his leg. He walked with a severe limp and with severe pain when he was on his feet for any length of time.

Five years later, another surgery in Salt Lake City on his Achilles tendon, performed by a talented young doctor finally allowed Barry to walk almost normally again.

Hanging over his head for the rest of his life, of course, is the unrelenting cost of his daily doses of immunosuppressive drugs and the ever-present chance of rejection—all of which we knew would be a part of a transplant but which is nevertheless an ongoing challenge with which to deal.

Though I still often experience a heaviness of soul, the legacy of comfort that came during that never-to-be-forgotten life flight quiets my mother's heart, and I continue to try hard to "trust in the Lord with all my heart and lean not to my own understanding."

A TIME FOR TRAVEL

ON THE ROAD AGAIN

For those of us who love traveling, there are few joys in life that equal the call of the open road.

The beginning of every trip is a fresh and new "Hello"—mostly to places we have never been but also to favorite spots we have seen before. As the words to Willie Nelson's popular tune say: "Going places I have never been; seeing things that I may never see again ... I can't wait to get on the road again." Over the years, Willie's song has become Dean's and my own theme song.

Early in our marriage, It was necessary for me to say one of my most difficult "goodbyes" to my dear parents who remained in Pennsylvania when Dean and I packed almost everything we owned in our small French Peugeot and headed West to make our new home. It wasn't that we didn't love the beauties of Pennsylvania and the East; it was simply that we wanted to experience more of America, perhaps putting into place a variation on the "Go West, Young Man" theme. For us, it was "Go West, Young Couple, Go West."

Pretty gutsy for two young people who had not traveled all that much in the past.

After almost deciding en route to relocate in Flagstaff, Arizona, we pushed on to California. There, after a week of looking around, we chose the beautiful, mid-coast city of San Luis Obispo, nestled in the mountains, as our new home.

Dean was fortunate to immediately find a teaching job there.

Eight months after moving to SLO, our first son, Glenn, was born, and this little guy traveled across the U.S. with us on three round trips to visit all four of his grandparents before he was 18 months old.

Then the opportunity came for us to take an administrative job with an American school in Western Samoa. Going there was a phenomenal adventure, one of many such adventures that stimulated a life-long and intense interest in travel. Not just the mosquitoes bit us in our two years there, but the travel bug as well.

While in Samoa we sent home several articles about our experiences to a small, local paper in Pennsylvania, and they were all featured on the front page—our very first effort at travel writing, a career we did not pursue further until many years later.

Returning to California, we chose to live and work in many interesting places. All became part of our developing love of travel, and we experienced many wonderful "Hellos" and "Goodbyes" as part of that love.

Just one of those places was Fair Oaks, California, a suburb of Sacramento and an area vibrant in history and scenic beauty. Most of our child-rearing years occurred in this place, a time especially rich in our lives.

As the boys grew a little older, we saved up and took all five of them to Hawaii. We found some luggage on sale and bought seven brown, soft-sided pieces that were all alike but of various sizes. We were quite a sight walking through the various airports where we overhead one lady disparagingly say, "Can you imagine traveling with five kids?"

Did we care? No way. We loved it, had done it for years, and we continued to do so until they were all grown and gone. (Now we take our grandkids—one at a time—with us on trips).

On our trips, the boys were amazingly good travelers, given a few rumblings and grumblings from their father when they tried pushing the envelope now and again. We traveled far and wide with them, mostly on modest trips.

The summer before our oldest, Glenn, graduated from high school, however, we planned what we knew would be the last trip together for the seven of us before the boys began to meander into their own pathways of life. We took a "red-eye" night flight to the East Coast where we rented a car and traveled for several weeks. We had planned carefully to see all the historical sites we could fit in between visits to family and friends.

What a truly marvelous trip that was!

Interestingly, nearly twenty years later, our oldest son, Glenn, decided to replicate that same kind of experience with his own family. This occurred the year before his oldest headed off to college.

Matthew, our second oldest, many years after that final trip we took with our five, said, "Going back East sparked in me an interest in politics and history, as well as traveling. It was the reason I later chose American Studies as my college major."

He says, "I remember the matching luggage we had. I remember the VIP tour of the Capital and the White House. I remember the Civil War sites we saw. I remember you and Dad always saying that memories, including family travels, are more important than *things*."

Following that trip, we moved to Southeast Idaho, mainly because of its close proximity to scenic destinations such as Craters of the Moon, Yellowstone, Jackson Hole, and the Grand Tetons.

Being educators, our income was never flush, and people would ask, "How do you find the money to travel, especially with a family?"

Our response was that we cut corners everywhere we could. We always had a comfortable home but not an expensive one. We usually bought good, second-hand furniture. We found a lot of the boys' clothes at garage sales and thrift stores. We bought food in bulk, ate out only once a week, and we thus saved for the trips we all came to love.

Even after our boys, one by one, left home, married and had families of their own, the two of us continued to fill our lives with travel.

After leaving our work in education, we further expanded our own travel opportunities by opening a travel agency, along with a school to train travel agents. This was a rather heady move for two people with little experience in the business world and little knowledge of the mechanics of the travel industry. However, we combined our love of teaching with our love of travel, and the business proved a success.

Because of it, we were able to take advantage of what are called "fam (or familiarization) trips." These trips are offered via fax or email by many cities, states, and countries to those working in the travel industry. The purpose is to acquaint travel agents with places the agents can then recommend to their clients.

During the years we owned the agency, we took advantage of these trips and traveled the globe. As we bid farewell to each destination, we knew we would have the fun of revisiting it again—probably only in memory—through the inevitable flashbacks that jump into our minds and/or the purposeful recollection of places as diverse as Canada's stunning Lake Louise and Banff, Helen Keller's home in Northern Alabama, Killyleagh Castle in Ireland's County Down, the exotic Amazon River, Israel, New Zealand, Australia, China, Japan, and lovely San Carlos, Mexico, to name just a few. Our favorite of all was Israel, a land of contrasts, great depth, great history, and great meaning to millions worldwide.

One year, after all our boys were out of the nest, Mom asked all five sons to write a letter to their dad on Father's Day for inclusion in a little "We appreciate our Dad" folder. Both of us were surprised that, in addition to expressing their love and gratitude for their father's positive influence in their lives, every single one said something to the effect: "Thanks, Dad, for all the trips."

Jokingly we say that few kids, ours included, would have said, "Thanks for the bathroom you remodeled," or "Thanks for putting in a new carpet," or "Thanks for buying that new car every year"(which we didn't do). Ours, of course, remembered seeing the Smithsonian Museums, traveling on old Route 66, crossing the Golden Gate Bridge, spending an entire day at the Polynesian Cultural

Center in Hawaii, and so much more. What they were saying, of course, is what dear, old Bob Hope used to say and sing: *"Thanks for the memories."*

That new piece of furniture will one day wind up in a garage sale. That deal that was so important to close will become less and less important. Kids won't remember if you mopped the kitchen every day or if you ironed that shirt to perfection, but family experiences shared in traveling together can, and usually do, last forever.

Now that our sons are raised, one of our priorities (as you already can tell) is to avail ourselves of every opportunity to take a grandchild with us to places near and far.

Never be afraid to say "Hello" to an opportunity to travel. The experiences travel provides can be one of life's greatest and most lasting treasures. To us, it's all so thrilling, so exciting, so wonderful, and I will be eternally grateful for the fact that my sweetheart and I have shared so much of it, virtually from the day we met.

Such a joy; such a blessing it has been in both our lives and that of our family.

Excerpted from our book *TRAVELING WITH GRANDKIDS* published by Cedar Fort Publishing, 2006.

POLYNESIAN SOJOURN

Ethnocentrism is a sociological term that means, in essence, "We are the best; our nation, our culture, is superior to all others."

This attitude seems a natural one for human beings, but a sad one when it precludes us from learning what other lands and peoples have to offer—especially the people of small, developing nations.

Few Americans, unfortunately, have the chance to live in remote foreign lands where they can see first hand how people in obscure parts of the world live their daily lives. Dean and I, however, were lucky enough to have this fabulous experience, and when we said "Talofa" (tah-LOW-fah), the Samoan word for "Hello" to our chance to go, our lives forever changed.

Three years after our marriage, while in our early twenties and teaching in Central California, the chance presented itself for Dean to accept a position as an elementary principal with an American school in the tiny Polynesian country of Western Samoa, now called simply Samoa. The first thing we said to each other was "Where is it?"

We knew it was in the South Pacific, of course, but we had to go to an atlas to pinpoint the miniscule group of islands located fourteen degrees south of the equator, mid-way between Hawaii and New Zealand. It looked so far away, yet the very name had a romantic appeal, and it seemed totally natural to simply say to each other, "Let's do it!"

From the start, the whole adventure sounded exciting, and it proved to be just that … and more.

Most Americans do not know that Samoa is composed of two separate countries. One is a protectorate of the United States called American Samoa. Its capital, Pago Pago, is the small port city where Somerset Maugham set his provocative short story, "Rain," and where two versions of the movie dealing with this same story were filmed.

Certainly the name of Maugham's story is apropos. It rains—and—rains—and rains—and rains in Samoa, particularly in the region of Pago Pago. The name of the city is pronounced "Pongo Pongo," and the word Samoa, as the natives say it, sounds like "Saw-MOW-ah."

The other group of islands comprising the independent nation of Samoa, with the main island of Upolu—only 20 miles wide by 40 miles long—was under the control of Germany prior to World War I, then became a protectorate of New Zealand, and finally an independent country in 1962.

The capital city is Apia, (pronounced Ah-PEE-ah). All the A's in the Samoan tongue are soft, and the language, though somewhat gutteral, is a pleasant one to hear spoken.

We found the Samoan people to be exceptionally hospitable and generous, even though quite poor. If you compliment a family on an item in their home, you will almost always find yourself taking it with you when you leave.

For example, I once admired a huge pineapple at a native friend's home. It must have stood 15 inches tall. Though I protested, I went home with the pineapple, and the family couldn't have been more pleased that I received their gift to me, even though I did so reluctantly.

The Samoan people are also full of fun and frivolity; they love to sing and dance and have feasts, and they never tire of sharing their fun with their guests—at least 99 percent of the time....

The only major character flaw we found among them generally, as a people, is a tendency toward an unreasoning temper that can flair with little provocation. A typical, though rare eruption can occur at various sporting events.

Rugby and soccer are the major national sports, along with volleyball, basketball, baseball, and cricket. At all of these competitive events emotions run high. If a perceived bad call is made, the spectators—men, women, and children, from both sides of the field, will rush onto the playing area en masse. We have then seen clubs or ball bats flying, with people's heads as the targets. Within minutes, the melee can subside, and a person who has been guilty of inflicting pain on someone else will quickly be sincerely apologetic and beg forgiveness.

Similar violence can be experienced if a child, or even a pig or some other domestic animal, is accidentally hit on the narrow roadways. Perpetrators—mainly non-Samoans—are advised that if they are ever involved in such an accident, they should **never** stop (as we are required to do under our laws) but immediately flee the scene, go to the nearest officer of the law and return with that figure of authority. Otherwise, an angry Samoan might have that seemingly uncharacteristic temper flare, club the motorist, and ask questions later.

Probably as more foreigners enter the country and make their home there, this type of occurrence may be less common. And certainly the positive characteristics of the natives far outweigh this rare, bizarre, and unusual phenomenon.

A wise traveler advised us early on, when in a foreign land, to "accept other cultures as they are, look for the best and 'flush the rest.'" We feel strongly that if more Americans came to adopt this attitude overseas, we would have less of the "ugly American" image and thus promote more international good will.

Since being in that remote country of Samoa for two years, we also feel that such an experience should be a requirement, of sorts, for those Americans who do not fully appreciate their homeland. We know this, of course, will never be the case. However, on our return to the U.S. we were shocked with the contrast of the wealth that exists here, even in the ghettos of our country. Our stay in a third world country made it seem to us that almost everything in America was bright and sparkling and clean, and the overall impression that hit us upon our return to the U.S. was that of a nation exuding richness as well as gross over consumption.

This is not to say that foreign lands are all poor and dirty. It is to say that America indeed IS rich and that Americans need to appreciate what they have more than they do. It pained us greatly to see Samoan children digging through the garbage cans of American families living in the islands. It pained us, also, to see people suffering from elephantiasis and other diseases related to poor sanitation and/or poor water drainage conditions.

Elephantiasis is a dreadful disease caused by the bite of large, striped mosquitos that we frequently killed. The ankles and lower legs of those infected swell to a hard mass as big as or larger than the thighs. Arms also swell, and the limbs remain huge. Fortunately, over the years, the World Health Organization has eradicated much of the disease.

As we think back to the beginning of our adventure, we remember well the day we left our San Luis Obispo, California, home and caught a bus for San Francisco. There were just the two of us and our little Glenn, who was 20 months old. We spent the night in one of the modest "City by the Bay" hotels, then took a taxi to the airport early the following morning.

Our only stop on the long air passage to Samoa was in Hawaii, and we spent a night on Oahu before catching our Pan Am flight to Pago Pago. Glenn was sick much of the way with frequent projectile vomiting. We were fortunate to have seats behind the bulkhead of the plane where he could rest in a crib and where we could better tend to his needs.

Gratefully, we landed near American Samoa's capital at 4 a.m. and were shocked to see that the airport building was only a ramshackle hut with dirt floors. We had to walk through deep puddles from a huge downpour to reach the single restroom serving everyone's needs.

Needless to say, our six-hour wait in the tropical heat seemed interminable. An additional shock was our first sight of the little prop plane that was to fly us 80 miles to the airport on the island of Upolu. There our plane landed on a grass air strip that we later learned on night flights was illuminated by Samoan boys and men holding torches as landing lights. The exoticism of that experience might have been fun, but we were just as happy to arrive on a bright Sunday morning. Travelers today fly into a modern Polynesian airport, so unlike what had awaited us.

Our immediate joy was seeing and smelling the brilliant green of the foliage and the bright reds and pinks and yellows of the hibiscus and other flowers on this stunningly beautiful island. Our host met us, helped us with our luggage, and we enjoyed our half hour ride along the winding coastal road. The ocean lapped the colorful shoreline, and the Samoan huts or "fales" (pronounced FAH-lays), lined the opposite side of the road. These traditional homes consist of an oval-shaped structure with palm-frond thatched roofs supported by poles. Woven mats can be lowered from the ceiling to form temporary "walls" when wind and rain necessitate. Otherwise, everyone and everything is in open view.

Modesty has a different meaning to the Polynesians, though this, too, is changing as our world becomes smaller. When we first arrived in Samoa, it was common to see people showering outdoors under a water pipe. Bare breasts among the women, especially the older women, were as common as the bare chests of the men. However, even in the open shower setting, women covered the lower parts of their bodies with the traditional lava lava—simply a two-yard piece of cloth wrapped around the body and tucked in at the waist to hold it in place.

The home where we were to live, unlike the fale, was more typically American. However, it, too, had no back door except for a screened one, and the windows were louvered and screened and were rarely closed. We, like the Samoans, preferred whatever cool air was available passing through our dwelling.

Dean referred to Samoa's two seasons as "hot and hotter" and "wet and wetter."

Having worked as a secretary in the communications office of Pittsburgh's U. S. Steel Corporation for a number of years, I had the habit of wearing nylon stockings every day. I felt I could never get along without them. However, in the heat of the tropics, I removed them the day we landed, and I never put them on again until the day we left two years later. My dress became the native loose, flowing muu-muu worn for both formal and casual wear. Dressy or casual thongs accompanied these cool gowns.

Dean told me he would "never be caught dead" in the Samoan male's traditional, skirt-like, wrap-around lava lava. He, too, invalidated his vows about what he would and would not do. Within twelve hours, his dress pants were in the closet, and he had adopted the lava lava and thongs, except for dress occasions when he did put on slacks and a shirt and tie and for school wear. First thing he did, however, upon arriving home from school each day was to shed his slacks and don one of his lava lavas.

There is so much humidity in these islands near the equator that lights burn year round in the major kitchen cupboards as well as in the clothes closets. Otherwise, bugs permeate the food, and green mold can appear in the shoes overnight.

A few of the Americans who came to work in the local schools suffered from culture shock. Manifestations of this very real "*dis-ease*" are compulsive washing of the hands, fear of mixing with the native people, and a sense of paranoia or panic. One or two families had to go home after only a week or two. They simply could not make the necessary adaptations. Most, however, did adapt and thrived on their experience. Thankfully, we were among the latter group.

And there were definite adjustments to be made. Hard-shelled cockroaches a half-inch wide and over an inch long were a common sight. So were hard-shelled black centipedes, also nearly a half-inch wide and sometimes five or six inches in length.

One night, as we turned down the light cover of our bed, one of the larger varieties of centipedes greeted us. It had pinchers that could flip up from its rear section and give a nasty bite. Luckily the sight of one occurred only once in our bed, but we did find several others in our house, along with fat, gray lizards, called peelees, that were sometimes six or more inches in length.

We found these critters too large and too squishy to kill. Besides they ate mosquitoes, and the Samoans told us they were the sign of a happy home. Be that as it may, we did not like the sight of them scurrying across our walls and ceilings, so we became adept at following along behind them with the brush end of a broom. We would chase them to the top of a doorway, then brush them to the floor and sweep them out the door.

Typically, they would exhibit their natural defense mechanism of dropping off their tails. The tail would go wiggling in one direction, and the lizard in the other. Later they would regenerate a new tail.

Once in our laundry hut, one of these delightful little fellows dropped from the ceiling down into the front of my muu muu. Needless to say, my scream could be heard from one end of the village to the other. I reached down, yanked it out and tossed it into the grass. The thought still makes me shudder, but I gradually came to look on such happenings as part of living in the heart of tropical Polynesia.

Surprisingly, and gratefully, no snakes have ever been found in Samoa.

The Pan Am jet came only once a week to American Samoa. It brought our mail, and how we looked forward to letters.

A sad event occured when our head principal learned his mother had died back in the States. He flew from our island to Pago Pago, stayed at a hotel where the alarm failed to waken him in time to catch his flight. He could do nothing but watch the huge plane take off, leaving him no choice but to return to our island, miss his mother's funeral, and wait another week to travel.

Dean and I and Glenn, as he grew, all came to love the Samoan children. They were obedient, friendly, and loving. We never tired of hearing them and their parents sing, and we were fascinated with the national dance, the sa-sa (saw-saw). We learned this dance and many of the country's songs, and we even had fun performing them at various events, along with our native friends.

We also came to love the food but abhorred the huge numbers of flies that inundated the pork, chicken, and fish dishes at a Samoan feast or fia fia (fee-ah fee-ah). Girls with palm fronds would wave them over the food, but the instant the fronds passed away from the food, the flies would blacken it once again. We greatly preferred indoor feasts.

Dean and I loved mixing not only with the Samoans but also the Chinese, New Zealanders (also known as Kiwis), and Australians (or Aussies) on the island, as well as the mixed races, including those of German ancestry.

Though we're not imbibers, we loved going to the White Horse Inn, a local bar and restaurant set in the hills above our home. Here we spent many weekend evenings dancing to the great band of Gerwin Keil, a descendent of the early Germans on the island.

Many of the New Zealanders owned local shops, and some of them looked down on the Samoans from whom they made their money. Though we became friends with some of the Kiwis, we disliked this attitude on their part.

Medical care in Samoa is socialized, and we considered the only hospital primitive in most ways. Even the locals feared going there "because it is a place to die," they often said and, indeed, the morbidity rate was high in the facility. A disturbing sight was seeing the surgical bandages, clothes, and towels, that had been washed in the river, hanging gray and stained on the clothes lines as one approached the hospital—not exactly an encouraging sight.

During our first year on the island, our teachers' village experienced an out-break of infectious hepatitis caused by sharing laundry facilities. Gamma globulin was flown in from the States to stop the spread. Anyone who contracted the disease was ordered to bed for a full month of rest. Unfortunately, Dean and I both did came down with it. Our skin and urine turned a brownish yellow, and we were quite weak for several weeks but recovered fully.

During Dean's brief stay in the hospital, the Samoan nurses found him fascinating, as a palagi (pah-LONG-ee) or white person. They were almost too shy to even give him a sponge bath and would just giggle when attempting to do so.

I, on an earlier occasion, sat on one of the long, outdoor benches awaiting my turn to see a nurse or doctor for a strep throat. All the patients waiting in line would remain seated, and each of us would gradually scoot our way toward the front desk. When I finally arrived at the examining station, a thermometer was popped into my mouth. A minute later, as I toyed with the vial, which I assumed had alcohol in it. I shuddered to see that the label read "RECTAL."

One of the New Zealand dentists abruptly left his job one day, when he reached his limits of frustration with the native people, after finding the workers using the sterilizer to cook some sausages for lunch.

In spite of such negatives, we felt we brought home with us much that was good in what we learned from the wonderfully warm human beings we came to love.

Among the Samoans, for example, we learned there is no stigma against illegitimacy. A child, thus born, is absorbed into the extended family unit. In fact, serious quarrels sometimes develop as to which set of grandparents or aunts and uncles will get the newborn to help raise.

In each Samoan village, a chief or "matai" is the ultimate authority. Other adults—parents, and principals, and teachers—are also greatly respected for their authority.

Older children are responsible for the younger ones, and this pattern of authority and of care and concern for any and all individuals in the community seems to only run into problems when these people move to countries, such as the U.S., where the Samoans sometimes say, "there is too much freedom." In other words, there is a delineation of authority and responsibility in their native land, and typically, when the Samoans move to America, this healthy pattern breaks down, and the people often begin to suffer from some of our rampant societal ills, including drug abuse. In fact, the toughest, most violent gangs in many U.S. cities are now unfortunately comprised of Samoans and Tongans.

As mentioned before, the Samoans are a loving, giving, people. It's interesting to watch teenage boys at dances. These muscular, handsome young men make sure there is no such thing as a "wall flower." It doesn't matter if a girl is pretty, or not so pretty, or fat, or whether she is shabbily dressed or well dressed. *All* the girls have a turn on the dance floor, and all have a great time. This never seems to be done out of a feeling of obligation; the boys just seem to see the concept of an evening of dancing from a totally different perspective—that of having fun and of inherently wanting to see everyone else have fun as well.

These are just a few examples of some of the intriguing cultural differences at play.

Though we were scheduled for a three-year term, Dean became ill again with what appeared to be the start of a second bout with infectious hepatitis. It was determined that he should be released from his contract and go for evaluation at a Stateside hospital. Thus we were forced to return home after just 22 months.

Like the famed author, Robert Louis Stevenson, we went to Samoa with the idea of sharing with the people there the wisdom and learning of the outside world. We did much of that and felt as good about our endeavors as, by all indications Stevenson did.

He, by the way, was revered by the Samoans. They called him "Tusitala," or "teller of tales." Suffering from ill health, he died there at age 44, and the Samoans carried his body to the top of a hill on the property of Samoa's head of state where the Samoans buried him in a stone crypt. The inscription on the grave is from the writer's own words:

"Under the wide and starry sky, dig my grave, and let me die. Glad did I live, and gladly die, and I lay me down with a will. This be the verse ye grave for me, here he lies where he longed to be. Home is the sailor home from the sea, and the hunter home from the hill."

Like this wise and learned Scotsman, we, too, came to appreciate the fact that the Samoan people have a profound wisdom and learning all their own. When it was time for us to say "Farewell" to Samoa and its people, Dean was well enough to gather with everyone in the school's huge gymnasium, following a fia fia or party where a roasted pig was served. It had been cooked in an underground umu (OO-moo). The entire feast was marvelous, and so many colorful leis were placed around our necks that the flowers covered our chins. Special small leis had been made for Glenn who was then almost four years old.

Then our beloved friends sang in their powerful, rich voices, in full Polynesian harmony, their traditional farewell song, "Tofa (toe FAH), my feleni," which means "Goodbye, my friend." It is a beautiful and touching song, and we could not hold back the tears.

The next day, our plane lifted off the island, and we looked down for the last time on its brilliant, astounding beauty. We understood we were going away from this incredibly beautiful place feeling good about our time of service there but also knowing that we had learned much more than we had ever been able to teach.

ALONE IN ANTARCTICA

Standing at the railing of the ship, MV Discovery, on a January evening, I found myself filled with a jumble of emotions I had never experienced. As we set sail from Antarctica's land's end and our four-day visit there, a huge sadness overcame me. For a rare hour, I was grateful to be completely alone on the deck, bidding farewell to the vast, white, silent continent.

Having traveled the world, I had been just a trifle reluctant to come here. Part of these feelings, I am sure, came from an admitted fear of the unknown. Part was thinking, as I had with the Orient before I went there, that this place was not really, as with some others, at the top of my list of places to go.

How wrong I was about traveling to both of these vastly different parts of our wondrous Earth.

Now, as I said a silent "Goodbye" to the bottom of the world, I found myself not wanting this soul-fulfilling experience to end. I realized what a rare privilege it was to have been able to come here.

As if, in response to my own feelings of farewell, the powdery, white clouds cleared to reveal the tallest black peaks of the peninsula, silhouetted against a pale, blue sky. The snow-capped mountains seemed to be silently regarding me in return.

It was 9:30 p.m. and still light and would be so until nearly midnight. Dressed in a sweatshirt and slacks, the almost summer-like temperatures of the Southern Hemisphere—nearly fifty degrees and a cool breeze—couldn't have been more pleasant. Seasons, of course, are the reverse of what we experience north of the equator.

This fantastic place seemed as pure and pristine as on the day of creation—snow endlessly white in color and the sea a penetratingly deep blue-black.

My experience has been that the best of friends I have known are often the quietest, with a wisdom that reveals much that is lying deep within. Such was my experience, as well, with Antarctica.

The immense icebergs receding from view, the depth of the dark ocean, the sight of white gulls, brown skuas, and some unknown black birds coasting close to the water, all overwhelmed me to the point of tears. The realization of the immensity of this vast, frozen desert left me grasping for words to even begin to give meaning to it.

I had walked among thousands of gentle gentoo and chinstrap penguins at the Argentinian and Chilean research stations on Deception and Half Moon Islands. I had watched seals and whales cavort in the frigid waters. I had viewed scenes of such incredible beauty as to defy description by camera or by word in this coldest, driest, and most remote place on the planet.

Meanwhile, I am certain I would not have liked coming here during the continent's winter season. Antarctica in the summertime, however, is a marvelously enriching experience—one unlike any other imaginable.

Eventually the stark, white continent faded from view, and I felt a poignancy like that of saying "Goodbye" to the dearest of friends. I was certain I would come here again only in memory, but those memories, so rich and vibrant, I know I will visit often in my mind and heart.

A TIME OF
GRANDPARENTS
& GRANDCHILDREN

FLYING KITES

◆

Why Grandparents are So Important

"We can do no great things: only small things with great love."
Mother Theresa

This thought from a woman renowned for her love for humanity could well apply to the fine art of grandparenting—and, rest assured, it is an *art* to be a good grandparent. As with any of life's major endeavors, developing this art of *grand* parenting takes time ... and patience ... and effort. It's an endeavor where few of us will truly do great things, but we *can* do small things with great love. That, of course, is what makes the process so fun and exciting ... because those small things can have such a lasting and important influence.

We remember the day that dear, little Tyler, our first grandchild, entered our lives. All of a sudden, we experienced a wonderful, new extension of ourselves. We realized that this extension will perpetuate itself for generations and generations to come. Suddenly, a part of *us*, in this mortal sphere and in the life to come, is now eternal.

Now that our own child is raised and has produced his own offspring, we gain a whole new perspective. In a way, as grandparents, we get another crack at making a difference. Looking back on our parenting experiences, we can see what effect the teaching of morals, values, manners, and education, in general, can have. We realize how much impact all of these teachings can have on the family and society.

Having seen and understood all of this, now we, as grandparents, can benefit from our often "got-too-late-schmart" kind of knowledge. We have what amounts to a second chance to help shape the lives of our posterity, even though not in as direct a way as we did as parents.

We might ask just what the word grandparent means? The dictionary says the obvious. It's the mother or father of one's mother or father—the older generation (yes, like it or not, that's us). The word also denotes "someone higher in rank, status, or dignity than others having the same title, such as grand duke or grand parent."

Simply by definition, we, as **grand** parents, do have "rank, status, and dignity." We are "grand" now, and we "oughta begin acting that way."

There's a plaque carved into the stone wall of an ancient castle in Scotland. The words have profound meaning for anyone in any role in life. They say: "Whate'er thou art, act well thy part."

As a grandparent, each of us has a new role to play—a new part to act—and an important one it is. Therefore, even if we think we're too young—or maybe even too old—to act that part, it's time to shape up and say, "I am a **grand** parent, and I'm going to do everything I possibly can to 'act well the part' that I'm now playing at this stage in my life."

That part, is after all, one that can and should be remembered with joy by our grandchildren. Most of us have only a few wonderful years to do our "acting well." Yet, grandchildren are often heard to say, "My grandmother was so special," or "I still remember wonderful times with my granddad." Much of these kinds of engendered feelings will stem from the efforts put forth.

So, if we want to remain with love in the memories of each and every grandchild, how do we help make this happen?

As a starter, think about the wonderful old story about the family who left all the cares and concerns of the day and went to fly their kites. Forever after, each member of the family tucked that marvelous memory away and drew it out when things got bad, as things do in everyone's lives.

One of the sons from that family became a prisoner of war, the grandmother lost her husband, a daughter had difficulties raising her child, yet each looked back on that fabulous day when they left all the things they "needed to do" go by the wayside and went out into the glorious April sunshine and flew their kites.

We all need to do this. We all need to leave the cares of the day and go fly kites or do whatever to create a memory such as this.

As grandparents, we often have more of an opportunity to take this kind of time than parents can do. We can go on walks with our grandchildren, take them to the best of movies, or on trips short or long. We can go to the zoo, read a book, sail boats on a pond, and, yes, we can even go fly kites with them.

Imagine the memories we can create. Imagine what will be conjured up in the minds of each grandchild when life gets hard. Imagine the legacy we can leave.

Those words from Mother Teresa are apropos:

"We can do no great things: only small things with great love."

NOT JERRY BELNAP

This is a little story we like to share with our teenage grandchildren:

It was a hot afternoon, and a few of us were wrapping things up for the day at the office.

The brief conversation started when I, as one of the owners of our small business, brought up the subject of the work habits of different people and how they can affect a company.

"It's true," said one of our co-workers, Michael Van Brunt. "Many of the kids coming out of school today don't have the same work ethic of even a generation ago. Statistics are showing that lots more have tried drugs and a good percentage are addicted."

"Mike, that may be true," Natalie, the other co-worker present (and one of our daughters-in-law) interjected, "But I really don't think that since you and I graduated from high school that things have changed all that much,"

"You may be right," Michael agreed. "However, I remember that time all too well," he reminisced. "Even those of us who were regular church-goers didn't come through those years without at least a few problems along the way. The temptations to do things we knew weren't right were always in front of us—and I feel certain that it's even harder for the kids now than it was then. Just about everybody I knew did something that wasn't "right on" back then, if you know what I mean."

As these two younger workers talked, I just sat back and listened.

After a minute or two Natalie said, "But, Mike, I think you're forgetting someone special when you say that *all the kids* were a little less than perfect—or at least a little less than they could have been." Then she paused and said, "… But not Jerry Belnap."

"You're absolutely right," Mike reflected. "How could I have forgotten Jerry?" as he recalled a young man both he and Natalie had known in high school.

"Not Jerry Belnap," he repeated thoughtfully, as he remembered this friend from past years.

Both Mike and Natalie continued to talk about this special classmate who was a popular young man, the oldest child in a family of ten, the quarterback star of the football team, a member of the school's 120-voice choir, and a good student.

"You know," said Mike, "Jerry never told an off-color joke—even in the locker room. He never got involved improperly with the girls, he never touched drugs, let alone a cigarette. In fact, he never even came any closer to swearing than saying, 'Darn."

Natalie laughed.

That's exactly how I remember Jerry," she said, as these two friends went on reminiscing about their friend.

I thought to myself. "What a great legacy one young man left for everyone who knew him."

Then I couldn't help but also ponder how wonderful it would be—as we all live our lives—if we could try to leave behind that same kind of legacy.

STORY LETTER TO A GRANDCHILD

◆

"About the Little Stinker"

Once upon a time there was a little girl who lived in a little college town far away from where you live, in another part of the United States. She had brown hair that shown with highlights of gold when the sunlight played on it. Her father said her blue eyes were like the ocean, deep and filled with brightness and beauty. She was thin and had the energy of a bouncing ball. She was smart and creative and born into a home where these qualities were encouraged. She was blessed to have a family who loved her—two parents who cared for her and an older brother and sister.

The little girl grew and grew.

When she was eight, her mother gave her some paper dolls, and for the next few years, nothing made her happier than cutting out the dolls and their clothes, designing and coloring new outfits, and spending hours with her best friend, Mary. Both girls lived in a paper doll world.

Wintertime brought snow balls, and ice skating, and walks in the winter wonderland of their small community. Fall walks were fun, too, kicking the crimson and gold leaves and hearing the crunch of them on the hard sidewalks or in soft dirt paths in the nearby woods.

"I want to go swimming," was the cry of this young girl as soon as the sun had warmed the lake enough in the summertime.

"Alright, but you need to dust and run the vacuum first," was her mother's response.

The little girl worked long and hard to do the best job she could with the housework, sometimes spending several hours to earn the joy of swimming and also earn the small amount of money needed to go to the one movie theater in town.

But swimming was her major summer passion. Sometimes she would swim in the morning, dash home, change clothes for lunch, then an hour later put on her wet bathing suit, and head back into the chilly waters of the lake again.

As she grew older, her father would say, "Come on, honey, let's read a book." and the little girl would sit near the father she loved and listen intently to the sound of his deep voice reading "Tom Sawyer," "Treasure Island," or some other exciting tale. They were stories she would remember all her life.

Sixth grade brought Girl Scouts, and it also brought a change in the little girl—the inevitable change from little girl to young woman—a change that often brings with it mood swings and an adjustment to the reality of life as it will eventually be in adulthood. She grew taller still and sometimes felt awkward with all the changes that becoming a young woman were bringing into her life.

"I don't wanna do this or that," she would complain.

"I don't like you anymore," or "Someday you'll be sorry," or even nastier comments to her parents and brother and sister and sometimes even her best friend.

"You mustn't talk that way to your mother," her father would scold her now and again. And in secret, never allowing her daughter to know her own feelings about these problems, her mother would say to her father, "I don't know what I'm gong to do with her."

"Now, now, she'll grow out of it," Father would assure her.

"I wonder," her Mother would reply when the two of them were alone.

As time went on, the young girl got into the habit of becoming moodier and moodier. In fact, she became downright unpleasant to live with—not always—but at times. Her nastiness made everyone in the family unhappy. Nastiness, of course, has a way of doing that. Unfortunately, dark moods spread and make everyone else feel the negative effects.

Boys, of course, go through something like this as well. They rough-house, knock each other around, sometimes get sassy or coarse in their talk, and can be generally unpleasant. It all seems to be part of coming of age, and some young people weather it better than others. The question then becomes why this is so—and how best to cope with it.

In this young girl's case, something happened to make this transition to early adulthood quicker and easier than it otherwise might have been. This occurred in her early teens.

First of all, you have to understand this was, as we said, a smart young girl who earned good grades in school and who learned quickly. Bright and intelligent, she was eventually able to pick up on what was needed to move her along through life and head her toward happier days.

"I can do that," is the attitude she had toward most of the challenges facing her as she grew up. It was an attitude her parents had always tried to engender in her. Yet the moodiness and sassiness seemed to grab hold of her too often, and it was obvious something had to change—and change quickly—in order for her and her family to be on a reasonably even keel again.

That change came about because her parents decided it was time to talk to her in a way they had never talked to her before.

Instead of the threats and reactions that had been part of the way they had tried dealing with things, they both sat down with their daughter one quiet afternoon. They waited for a special day when she was in a good mood, and this was important too, because trying to reason with a young person who is in one of those other kinds of moods can be like talking to the proverbial wall.

"Sweetheart," Dad started out by saying, "Your mother and I want you to know how very much we love you."

The girl looked at the father she loved in return, and a shy little smile danced across her lips. Silently she thought to herself, "Okay, what's this all about?"

The father noticed that little smile and said, "Honey, did you know that a smile is just about the nicest gift you can give anyone? It doesn't cost anything, but it's value to others is of special worth. It makes other people happy; it brightens their day, and you know something? You have just about the sweetest smile of anyone I know."

The girl looked into her father's eyes and couldn't help letting her smile grow just a little broader than it had been before.

Then her mother said, "We just felt we needed to share a few thoughts with you today, sweetheart. They are important, and they can have great meaning to you throughout your life—if you will let them work in your mind and heart."

Mother looked at Dad, and they both looked at the daughter who meant the world to both of them ... even though she didn't realize how much at the time.

Mother continued, "Think about this, if you will, for just a minute. You and your father and I only have a few years left before you grow up and leave us, and each of those years will go by just a little faster than the one before. It's really mostly up to *you* to determine what our home is going to be like during those few years ... whether it will be heaven or hell."

Mother paused and let her words hang in the air. It's true that sometimes silence can have much more meaning than talking. Besides, "hell" wasn't a word Mother used very often.

"You understand what your mother is saying, don't you?" Dad asked, and with pursed lips, the young girl looked out the living room window and shook her head that she did.

"Keep in mind," mother continued, "that none of us is guaranteed tomorrow."

Somehow the words her parents spoke went straight to this wise young girl's heart. In that heart, she realized what her parents were trying to convey to her, even though she didn't want to admit that she did.

Putting her parent's counsel into action made sense, but the change, of course, didn't happen all at once.

Her junior high and senior high school years did speed by, and she had many happy experiences both at school and at home, in part because she began to put into practice, as best she could, her parent's advice. She had a few times when she slipped into her old grouchy skin, but most of the time, she made a conscious effort to smile and be kind to everyone, but especially to her own family. Her brother and sister, who were several years older, meanwhile had left home and married.

Her graduation day from high school was extra special. Her parents gave her a red rose to carry as she received her diploma, and she had a wonderful date after the ceremony with the young man she was to marry a few years later.

Not much time passed after her graduation until one unforgettable night when she was to remember so vividly the words her mother had spoken years before: "Be careful how you treat those you love, because no one is guaranteed tomorrow."

The day began with her father giving her mother a big kiss in the kitchen. He was leaving on a business trip. He also kissed his daughter and gave each of them a big hug. They all smiled as they waved "Goodbye."

The family this man loved so dearly was never to see him alive again. He was killed that same evening in an automobile crash. The loss seemed more than any of them could bear. However, as he had taught them how to live and love each other, so he had, in his own special way, taught them how to go on living after he was gone.

They all felt that the greatest blessing they carried with them was that the last gift they gave each other were smiles.

As her dad had often said, "It's easier to smile than to frown. It's easier to be kind than to be mean. Life really can be like heaven on earth, if everyone will just put forth a little extra effort to make it so."

Can you guess who the girl in the story might be? If you guessed your Grandma Nancy, you're right. And my wish for you, in your sojourn on this earth, is one of joy and happiness always. One sure way to make that happen is to put forth the effort to be kind to those you love the most and, even when times get hard, not to be a "little stinker," as I once was for a time but to do your best to just ***keep smiling***.

CHOOSE TO BE A LADY; CHOOSE TO BE A GENTLEMAN

I often hug my grandchildren and tell them how much I love them. Each one represents a bright, new "Hello" to this great, old world. They will always be a part of me ... and I a part of each of them.

If I could, I would shelter them from all that is harmful, and evil, and wicked in the world but, instead, I can only caution them and trust in their abilities to focus on that which is good, and right, and wonderful about their turn on earth.

I would ask each of my granddaughters to always be a lady—each grandson to be a gentleman. I would say to each, "For your own joy and happiness ... and that of those around you:

- Hold your head high. Be proud that you are a child of God.
- Love God with all your heart, might, mind and strength.
- Be kind and loving to others, especially those who are downtrodden.
- Walk, talk, sit, and act like the royal person you are.
- Listen to the counsel of your parents; they love you beyond measure.
- Be forgiving of yourself, when you make mistakes—and forgiving of others.
- Constantly strive to learn, and grow, and improve your mind.
- Treat your body like the temple it is; keep it clean and neat and free of tattoos and such.
- Dress and act modestly. Never be "cheap."
- Buy quality clothes; they last longer and look better.
- Keep your room in order and as a place where the Spirit can dwell.

- Date and marry the kind of person you can be proud to take anywhere.

- Live above the crowd.

- Use your time wisely. As Benjamin Franklin said, "Do not squander time; it is the stuff life is made of."

- Choose to fill your wonderful mind with that which is uplifting.

- Choose to read the best books and see the best films.

- Use good language; foul language can easily become a bad habit.

- Some things really never change: Each generation thinks they are discovering the difference in the sexes for the first time. Be moral in your conduct.

- Young men: Honor girls and women. Never be a part of locker-room talk. Regarding your personal moral conduct, read and study the stories of Joseph and David in the Bible. For your life-long happiness, ***Be a Joseph.***

- Young women: Be the kind of girl deserving of a young man's honor. ***Be a Rebekkah, a Deborah, a Ruth, a Mary.*** Never allow your name to be one of those bandied about in a demeaning way. Keep your standards high.

- Remember that what matters most is what lasts longest.

- Always remember, too, how much you are loved by your parents, your grandparents, and your Father in Heaven. All wish only life's best for you, so please, please, please:

CHOOSE to Be a Lady! CHOOSE to Be a Gentleman!"

A TIME OF ENDINGS

THANKSGIVING

"Sometimes I think that maybe it's really all about the little things," I said to my husband as we took our early morning walk.

"Meaning what?" he replied, long ago used to my often cryptic remarks.

"Being thankful for the little things, especially as we come to the end of the road," I said.

"Such as?" he asked.

I laughed and felt almost foolish as I replied, "Well, this morning, to begin my day, I was grateful for a toothbrush and toothpaste and a warm cloth to wash my face. And through the day, I often think about all the many material blessings we enjoy—everything from washing machines and indoor plumbing to our food and facial tissues, pens and pencils, clean bed linens, books, and good music, and on and on—things that we take for granted every day ... and those intangibles like the greetings and smiles of people we know ... and people we don't know, special hugs and kisses from those we love, compassion, forbearance, laughter and song, and all that's so much a part of every day."

"Never really thought about it all like you have," he mused. "That's a lot to be pondering."

We walked on in silence, enjoying our time together and entertaining our own thoughts, as we had done for many years. My musings included many things that morning—some of them repeat thoughts that had often entered my mind.

So many times, as I wash my hands, I am grateful for water and a bar of soap. It's not simply cleanliness involved in this ritual, although cleanliness is itself a blessing. There is also the symbolism of the washing away past mistakes and indiscretions.

A scripture in the Book of Psalms reads, "Who shall ascend into the hill of the Lord? or who shall stand in his holy place? He that hath clean hands and a pure heart.; who hath not lifted up his soul unto vanity, nor sworn deceitfully."

Being able to wash away dirt and sweat from my hands is, to me, a act of refreshing and a reminder to periodically renew myself mentally and spiritually.

Having had the opportunity to travel the world, and often being hosted in the loveliest of surroundings, I am nevertheless happiest and most content with the simpler things of life. I have thought many times that three of the greatest blessings of life are shelter from the elements, food to eat, and someone to love who loves me in return.

I'm so glad there's a national holiday written into our law and set aside specifically to give thanks to God for all that we have.

Dean interrupted my musings with, "Being able to walk together is kinda special, too," he said, taking my hand in his.

I felt glad, as was often the case, that we were on the same wave length—this time that of gratitude.

Having two sons who, for different reasons, cannot walk with ease and often only with pain, I think of them so much when my own body carries out this kind of exercise that brings joy to my soul. My eyes often fill with silent tears when I think of them and of others who must spend their lives dealing with both physical and mental adversities that are not mine to bear. We all have our share of adversities, it's true, but I believe it's important to try to empathize with others whose burdens are different from our own.

Further thoughts carried me to that obscure and puzzling concept mandated in the scriptures of giving thanks to God in all things. How does one give thanks *in all things*? I can only conclude that everything that we go through in our lives gives us experience and that through experience, both good and bad, we grow. This idea would fit with something Albert Einstein once said—to the effect that this world is a "school," a place where we are to learn, and grow, and develop ourselves.

Corrie ten Boom, a Dutch woman who survived the Nazi concentration camps, is remembered for once saying to her younger sister, Betsy, who died in the camps, "How can you be so positive? Surely you can't be grateful for the lice and bugs that crawl on our bodies?" To which Betsy replied, "Oh, Corrie, even here there's a blessing. The bugs keep the guards away from us."

Gratitude has been referred to as the noblest of virtues, and many consider ingratitude a sin—a remarkable contrast and something to ponder. I shared some of these thoughts with Dean as we neared the end of our walk.

"It certainly isn't easy to give thanks when everything seems to go wrong—especially when someone we love or when we ourselves are hurting," was his comment.

"Another of life's challenges," I replied, "but a philosophy that surely lifts us to a higher plane of thought."

We climbed over a low fence and leaned back to rest for a few minutes. Then, as we neared the end of our walk, I took Dean's hand once again.

"I'm grateful for you," I said. "I'm grateful to have had good parents and a brother and sister that were such a big part of my life—for our sons and their wives and families."

As we entered a home now devoid of all the noises of our lively family of boys, Dean gathered me in his arms and gave me a hug and a kiss.

"I love you," he said.

"I love you, too, I replied, "and thanks …"

A LEGACY FOR THOSE HE LOVED

Before dawn on a rainy August morning in Pennsylvania, a loud knock came at the door.

My mother, wakened from a sound sleep, gathered her loose robe about her and was shocked to see a uniformed police officer standing on the porch.

"Is this the home of Robert McVeigh?" he asked.

"Yes," my mother answered, "but there are two Robert McVeighs—my husband and my son."

"This is in regard to a Robert McVeigh who was traveling in New York state. He's been killed in an auto accident."

My mother screamed and nearly fainted.

There had been no preparation, no "I'm sorry we have bad news; would you like to sit down?" Only a curt, sharp, devastating sentence to end 38 years of marriage and introduce my mother all too abruptly to the long, lonely halls of widowhood.

A neighbor across the street had been awake and heard the scream. She hurried over to learn the devastating news. Only 61 years old at the time of his death, he had been a vibrant, loving and devoted husband and father. As a family, we had all loved him beyond measure.

He was the first in our immediate family to die, and his loss was overwhelming—especially to my mother who had stood by his side for 38 eventful and fulfilling years of marriage.

Dean and I had traveled earlier that same day to visit his parents who lived two hours away. Watching the evening news at their home, we learned of a fatal automobile accident just north of the state line. The name of the victim was not released, and everyone went to bed as usual.

In the middle of the night, a call came that there had been an accident and that we were to return to Pittsburgh right away. Leaving baby Glenn with his paternal grandparents, we quietly drove though the gentle nighttime rain. The night was dark, and few words were spoken.

168

"I pray he's alright," I said, leaning my head on Dean's shoulder. Neither of us wanted to think the worst, and neither of us connected the evening news seen earlier with our loved one.

At dawn, when Dean and I arrived at the house, I ran from the car into the entryway of our home. My mother, totally distraught, ran toward me and screamed, "He's dead, Nancy, he's dead."

Those words crushed my heart, and I will remember the shock of them forever.

I gathered my mother in my arms and tried to comfort her incredible sorrow.

My sister, Mary, meanwhile, was in her home in New Jersey with her husband, Ken, who could not sleep that night. He was standing by the phone when the call came. He gently woke Mary, and she knew immediately that something terrible had happened.

"It's Dad," was all she said.

The two of them, had driven the eight hours on the Pennsylvania Turnpike just the day before, following a visit to our family home. Immediately, they drove the distance again in the opposite direction heading back to Pittsburgh.

Our brother Bob had also left that Monday morning on a business trip in the southern part of the state. Once the body was brought back to Pittsburgh, it was young Bob, the only son, who was called on to perform the gruesome task of identifying his father. He had loved his father dearly but, as with many of us, he never realized just how much until death pulled him violently away from us.

"What will I ever, ever do without him?" my mother asked over and over again. With her children all grown and married and with families of their own, we knew the adjustment would be the most difficult of all for her. However, she and our dad had planned well for this eventuality and had discussed its inevitability many times. She was as prepared as anyone could be for a transition in her life for which no one could ever truly prepare. Our hearts ached for her.

Dad had been on the road almost weekly in his work as a salesman. Traveling from our home that final day, he had journeyed from Pittsburgh, Pennsylvania, to a small community just over the New York state line near Jamestown. It was there, on a slick, rainy road that his car veered off the gravel shoulder.

Two nurses in an oncoming vehicle reported that the green Ford simply skidded off the wet highway. Its single occupant, in pre-seat belt days, was thrown from the vehicle, his head hitting one of the guardrails at the side of the road.

Because of these circumstances, a viewing of his remains was not possible, and we later felt this was for the best since we were able to remember him as we had last seen him.

Saturday morning, before the accident, Mother and Dad, my sister, brother and I gathered at a photographer's studio for our first family photo in over 15 years. Since I lived in California and my sister, Mary, lived in New Jersey, we did not all get together as often as we would have liked with our parents and our brother and his family, who lived in Pittsburgh.

However, that Saturday was one we would always remember fondly. Dad and our brother, Bob, were the "cut-ups" of the family, and they had the photographer—and all the rest of us—in stitches. The saddest part was that Dad would never live to see those exceptionally fine photos the rest of us now treasure so much.

The next day, Sunday, we shared Church services together followed by one of Mother's fabulous meals, then a relaxing time just visiting with each other. In the afternoon my sister and her husband said their goodbyes and returned to New Jersey, and my brother and his family were off to their home as well.

Early Monday morning, Dad ate his customary eggs, toast, and juice and made ready to be off on another week of business. He always hated to leave and postponed his departure as long as he could. Finally, however, standing in the kitchen he gathered Mother inside his raincoat and gave her a big hug and kiss.

"I'll miss you," he told her softly.

"I'll miss you too," she replied. "It gets harder all the time to see you go."

It was difficult for me to imagine one of them without the other. I loved them both so much.

"Don't I get a kiss, too?" I teased, seeing he was ready to leave.

He laughed and gave me a squeeze and a kiss on the cheek, then hurried to the car. He turned to wave as the pale green Ford sloshed away in the August rain.

In retrospect, I have often thought how much I treasure this last memory of him. It's a rare family, as we all know, that doesn't have its share of spats and quarrels. Our family certainly was no exception. However, a simple, little poem comes to mind that applies to that particular morning in our lives. It's called "Our Own," written by Margaret Elizabeth Sangster:

> If I had known in the morning,
> How wearily all the day
> The words unkind would trouble my mind
> That I said when you went away,
> I had been more careful, darling,
> Nor given you needless pain;

But we vex our own with look and tone
We might never take back again.

For though in the quiet evening
You may give me the kiss of peace,
Yet it well might be that never for me
The pain of the heart should cease.
How many go forth in the morning
Who never come home at night?
And hearts have been broken for harsh words spoken
That sorrow can ne'er set right.

We have careful thought for the stranger,
And smiles for the sometime guest,
But oft for our own the bitter tone,
Though we love our own the best.
Ah, lip with the curve impatient,
Ah, brow with the shade of scorn,
'Twere cruel fate were the night too late
To undo the work of morn.

Thinking back to that day in our lives, all of us are eternally grateful there was no "work of morn" to undo and that our final memories have become a beautiful picture in time—a reminder to be gentler and kinder to those we love on an everyday basis.

The news of his death shattered us, yet there was at the same time a peace that surrounded us because of the strength he had built into us and the knowledge he had ingrained in us that we would all be together again when this brief time of testing and trial is finished.

The greatest blessing, strangely, was yet to come when his luggage was returned to our home a few days later. It had not been disturbed, and in unpacking it we found a brown, spiral binder containing Dad's journal.

None of us had been aware that he had even been writing it, although my sister had always encouraged him to do so. She often said what an interesting life he had lived, and she wanted him to write about it for his children, grandchildren, and great-grandchildren.

In opening and reading it, tears flowed freely. It wasn't particularly long and involved, but it conveyed to us, in his own special way of writing, his thoughts on the life he had lived, his own fears, frustrations, hopes, and joys and his unspoken commitment to us all.

Strangely, at the end, he had in essence brought it to a close with these truncated thoughts: "Nancy's marriage and departure for California—Trips to the Atlantic shore—Wonderful active life and fine family—No regrets—Full life—Four wonderful grandchildren and Nancy expecting—What more could one desire? Sarah and I now alone …"

Dad's heart had not been good and he had taken nitroglycerin tablets for years. Perhaps he knew better than we did how near the end actually was. The supposition regarding the accident was that he had in all likelihood had a heart attack at the wheel. We have always been grateful no one else was involved.

From the thankfully retrieved journal my sister later extracted and amplified a full-fledged biography of his life, which she published under the title *Sojourn*. Had she never done this, the journal, in and of itself, would still have been a legacy for all generations of his family to enjoy.

People say they could never write a book. However, just one page a week recapping life experiences can soon evolve into a book. The grammar, spelling, and punctuation are insignificant when compared to a life story told.

If it's never done, as is the case with the vast majority of people, then within a generation or two, there is nothing to represent a life lived except for dates on a tombstone, and these, too, usually only last for a hundred years or so at best.

Writing a journal or a life story helps all of us focus on the important things of life and can distill for us the deepest of human emotions. A journal can also be a legacy for those we love, as our father's was for us.

NOT IN THE WINTER, LORD

The call came on January 15.

"Nancy, our Mother's gone."

I was standing in the kitchen of our California home as my sister told me that our mother had died just an hour before in her home in New Jersey.

Unlike our father's death which had been so sudden and so violent—and in a summertime auto accident—Mother had been sick for seven, long years. During those years, she had suffered with nephritis, or kidney disease, and we had anticipated this day for a very long time.

During all those years, the unspoken dread uppermost in my mind was that she might die in the winter time, and I had silently prayed over and over again: "Not in the winter, Lord. Please don't let her die in the winter."

I felt I could handle her passing, but I did not believe I could stand to bury my mother in the snow.

My family and I had been living in California since my father's death nearly 14 years earlier, and I had come to love the sunshine and the warm climate. Though I had enjoyed wintertime as a child, I had conjured up the notion that I would not be able to bring myself to accept the idea of my Mother dying in the wintertime. My mind could only see the coldness and harshness of that season in which to lose someone so close to my heart.

After my father's death, Mother had traveled several times from Pennsylvania to California to help with the births of our sons and just to visit. It had been wonderful to have her with us.

Then, at age 68, she became ill and could no longer travel. While living near my brother and his family in Pittsburgh, she became one of the first patients to endure the rigors of kidney dialysis. The severity of her situation eventually necessitated that she live in a nursing home near the University of Pittsburgh Hospital. All of us in the family visited her as often as we could.

Toward the end of her life, the procedures for dialysis had improved enough that she no longer had to be tied to the University of Pittsburgh. It was then determined that she live with my sister and her family in New Jersey where she could travel to a nearby hospital every three days for her dialysis treatments.

"I'm doing pretty good," was her usual comment when I spoke with her so many times on the telephone.

She complained very little, but we all knew the treatments drained her terribly. Just when she began to get a measure of strength back, she was due for another cleansing of her blood now that the work of her kidneys had ceased. Shunts inserted in her veins to enable the treatments were painful, and the sites sometimes became infected. These sites had to be changed frequently.

I felt especially helpless, in the situation, living so far from her.

"I just pray she doesn't die in the winter," I began to confide now and then to Dean who understood.

As each springtime came, I was relieved thinking that surely she would leave us before the next winter season in the East would come.

Then, finally the call did come—and the immediate weather reports in the East were terrible—ice, and cold, and ... and snow.

"I'll stay here with the four youngest boys, and you take Glenn with you," Dean suggested.

We both agreed this would be the best plan, so within a day I was able to buy a warm, winter coat which I had not needed in years. I also bought a pair of trousers for our rapidly growing oldest son who was now almost 13 years old and who was to be one of the pall bearers. He looked quite handsome and grown up, and I was grateful he could be with me throughout this difficult time.

"I love you, honey," Dean said, as Glenn and I prepared to leave him at the airport.

"Take good care of your mother," he said to Glenn who shook his head that he would ... and he did.

I had not dreaded my mother's passing. We all knew she had endured long and well and that it was time. The dread had always been a burial in the snow, and Mother's funeral was held on one of the worst winter days any of us in the family had ever experienced. Only a few people were able to travel to the mortuary in Pittsburgh, and none were able to come from out of town. Fortunately our plane from California had landed two days prior, when travel was possible.

The few of us who could attend the brief but lovely service then followed the hearse holding our mother's remains to Pittsburgh's Highwood Cemetery and to the place where, years ago on a warm August afternoon, we had buried our father. This day, the winding road lead up the hill through the deep snow, which had been cleared enough to allow the small procession of cars.

Standing by Mother's grave side that cold, gray, blustery, January day, a sudden, comforting feeling of warmth came over me. The feeling—a total and complete surprise on that bitter day—was as if I were being wrapped in a warm, woolen blanket.

That supernal feeling of warmth I felt was akin to an autumn day years earlier when I had come to visit my father's grave, the grave that I saw once more before me this day, beside my mother's burial place. I had not been to the cemetery since his death because of living so far away, and when I was finally able to go there once again, I experienced that same, warm feeling, even though the day was also cold.

That day was one of the only times I went to his grave because, as I stood looking down, it was as if my father whispered in my ear, "You don't have to worry about coming to visit this place, Nancy. I'm not here. Please remember that; I'm not here."

The same warm, comforting feeling was the one that surrounded me as I stood in the snow beside my mother's grave. All the dread was gone, and the prayer I had offered so many times was answered in a way I had never expected.

Through this experience—and many others throughout my life—I have learned that I can deal with adversities I never thought I could. I have learned that the strength comes to endure things I was certain would be impossible to endure.

In the end, seeing "through a glass darkly," perhaps this is what faith in God is really all about.

GROWING OLDER WITH DIGNITY

The process of growing older may be the best kept secret of all—what a challenge it is. As with the other stages of life, it's all about how we choose to live out those precious years of our lives before it's our turn to head over the rainbow.

Not all of us are blessed, of course, with the opportunity of growing old, but those of us who are must decide how we want to traverse those final years of our sojourn on the planet.

A wise person once said, "The golden years are laced with lead." My thinking is that, in spite of the inevitable lead that can be present, those years are nonetheless golden, or can be, depending on our circumstances, chosen and otherwise.

As with all the other stages inherent in our earthly days, we do have choices as to how we will live out our final ones. I personally remain eternally grateful for a father and mother who left me a wonderful legacy as to how this is done.

My mother and dad were Pennsylvanians of Episcopalian persuasion. Pennsylvania is where they lived and where they both died. My father died suddenly, and his last words were kind ones. His last act was a kiss for my mother. She lived another 14 years and never re-married. She often said, "I had the best." Some people place the words happily married in quotation marks, as if this is a play on words or, at worst, an impossible scenario. Well, 'taint! My parents taught me that lesson as well.

Mother suffered from kidney failure after Dad died. However, she kept her sense of humor to the end, showing us how to die as well as how to live.

In spite of the inevitable difficulties inherent in the close relationship of marriage, my parents, Bob and Sarah, had their priorities straight. Their relationship to their Maker came first, then their relationship to each other, then their family, next helping others along life's path, followed by earning a living, and finally their love of travel, reading, and other interests. I wish I could always keep my own priorities in as sharp a focus. This kind of focus makes such a huge difference throughout one's life.

Changes, as we age, are all part of the inevitable process, and as a woman, I applaud those of my own sex who, on occasion, to express their joy of living, wear jaunty hats, dangling earrings, long, flowing dresses, and just generally have a ball. I would rarely, if ever, do this, but I admire those who do.

Wonderful days of fun and humor are what makes life bearable, especially being able to laugh at oneself. Color in a wardrobe, color in life, and color in relationships, throughout our lives, are the things that make for contentment and happiness at any stage of existence. Surely we all need to take time to laugh and have fun because it helps so greatly in the aging process.

Then, I think, we need to keep working at something meaningful and also working at staying positive.

I also believe we, as women, have the responsibility of setting an example of dignity, of striving for all that is lovely in life, of kindliness and caring, of elevating ourselves above catty conversations (and I've found men can be just as capable of this as women), of enduring the inevitable trials and challenges life presents to all of us, of going forward with head high—and with the elixir of humor, as noted, ever capping off our days.

We can speak our minds at any age; that is our right. It is **not** our right to be unkind in the way we speak to others or about others, especially those closest and dearest to us. There isn't a person alive who cannot be hurt by unkind words. They sting, and they damage relationships.

Complete abandon in our speech and our actions is untenable, and the necessary restraints we place on ourselves at any age, particularly as we chug along through the last decades that life may grant to us, are part of the legacy we leave behind. For one, I'd rather grow old gracefully than disgracefully, as some would advocate.

The saddest scene, and one I see far too often, are old people on the streets whose lives have been wasted through alcohol, drugs, wanton living, or simply giving up on life. It's then I remember lines from John Greenleaf Whittier: "For of all sad words of tongue or pen, the saddest are these, 'It might have been.'"

Conversely, the poet Robert Browning once said, "Grow old along with me; the best is yet to be. The last of life for which the first was made." I agree. My parents taught me, through their supernal example, to agree.

How grateful I am for that precious gift they gave me of how to live and of how to grow old. My prayer has always been to set that same kind of example for my own posterity. To me, that's what life is all about.

Though shoulders begin to stoop, joints begin to ache, veins begin to show, and wrinkles announce the inevitability of time's hand in our lives; still it's onward, and upward, with a cheery heart.

PASSENGERS ONLY
BEYOND THIS POINT

Anyone who has traveled by air is familiar with a sign at every airport terminal that reads:

PASSENGERS ONLY BEYOND THIS POINT

In our travel writing work, Dean and I have seen this sign many, many times.

Both of us are well aware what it is to plan for a trip. We have been privileged to take countless trips throughout our own great nation and around the world. Because of this, we know all the details that go into the careful preparation for, and executing of, each journey.

I have often thought that most people, ourselves included, sometimes put more detailed planning in place for a trip, or a family reunion, or just a simple vacation than we do for our life's journey.

Most of us are familiar with setting a travel objective, determining and reviewing our itinerary, obtaining needed documents, inoculations, passports and visas, going over our packing lists, and being sure everything is taken care of at home before we leave.

Symbolically, do we take the time to cover the same kinds of bases in our life's journey and consider what will we leave behind when our sojourn in this "home" is over? Have we tried to live the kind of life that will be remembered for its goodness, its kindness and concern for others, its focus on God, relationships, and things of an eternally important nature? Will we have chosen the "better part"?

In short, will the planning and choices here on earth have prepared us to make that final and inevitable journey? Will we be ready when we see the sign ahead of us reads:

PASSENGERS ONLY BEYOND THIS POINT

YOU CAN GO HOME AGAIN

Thomas Wolfe was wrong. The title of his popular novel tells us, **You Can't Go Home Again**, but, in fact, **you can**. Wolfe would rob us of what is a right, a privilege, a duty, and a joy.

Some of us are lucky enough to return and see the actual physical surroundings of a home we once dearly loved. Others of us have to make the journey to this special place in our minds and hearts.

Our family home, for many years, was 8549 Sunset Avenue, a big ranch-style house in a suburb of sprawling Sacramento, California called Fair Oaks. The quaint little town is a gateway to historic Folsom, the gold rush city of Placerville, and the foothills of the Sierra Nevada Mountains.

Dean and I had been married fourteen years—most of them spent with Dean working his way through graduate school. We considered this our first real home, and we put much of ourselves into fixing it up and making it a place to raise our family, as we had dreamed of doing,

For twelve magical years we were a family there. In later years, some of us called it "Camelot," and, in many ways, that's what it was—certainly, at least, in memory.

Our "gentleman farm," as we sometimes called it, sat on two acres of rolling land. The house itself sat on the middle acre of the property, with a half acre in the front and another half-acre in the back.

Approaching the long, winding driveway from the south on Sunset Avenue, we traveled up a rather steep hill, then turned in to the left. From the other direction, when riding in our colorful Volkswagen van, we often careened rather speedily down around the sharp corner by the mailbox, and it was lucky we never turned the car over as we veered into the sloping driveway. Robb says he still remembers the clicking of the turning signal. Strange what memory brings back to each of us.

The curving driveway sloped down through a swale and then up again to approach the house which was situated on a knoll. Dead ahead, as we approached the house from the driveway stood a magnificent oak tree, symbol of the State of California, and symbol, too, of much that is good and strong.

It's illegal to fell an oak in California, and we found it interesting to learn that another huge oak graces the old Hoch homestead in the Oley Valley of Pennsylvania near Reading. That homestead has been in the Hoch name since it was built by our Swiss immigrant ancestor, Rudolph Hoch, and his son Johannes, in 1723. Though we never really thought about it when we lived in California, now I sometimes think of our oak as symbolizing the strength of our family and our home there, as well.

Nearer the house stood a fruit-bearing orange tree, a smaller lemon tree, and a large magnolia. The boys would sometimes pick the huge white magnolia blossoms and bring them inside to perfume the house; they also picked other flowers for Mom over the years, and she appreciated so much those gestures of love more than any presents they could have bought.

The sunlight seemed to walk across the lawns and right into the house. We had plenty of sunshine in Fair Oaks, and, like the John Denver tune, "Sunshine almost always made us feel high."

When we purchased the home, there were 17 almond trees on the property and a long row of pines near the east side of the house. The almonds produced an abundant crop of delicious, soft-shelled nuts, and it was the boys' job each year to place tarps on the ground and use huge, metal poles to knock the almonds and harvest them, using the money for Scout camp. We gave plenty away and ate the rest.

Through this and many other tasks around the place, each of our five sons learned that labor is the price paid for rewards of many kinds, including food, safe and pleasant lodging, schooling, progress, and happiness. The boys internalized the concept that it is only through work and effort that the greatest joys of life become ours.

Shortly after moving into this home, we placed a long, rail fence around the front pasture. It took 14 gallons of white paint to cover it, and the boys did this work, as well. The wooden portion of the house only took ten gallons.

We also put a lifetime aluminum roof on the place and had to make a decision regarding installing an air conditioning system or a swimming pool. You can imagine which way the family vote went on that issue.

To save funds, we learned the ins and outs of sub-contracting our lovely kidney-shaped pool, first scheduling the "dig man," then the "steel man," then the concrete pourer, then the tile and deck workers, and so forth. We chose a rich-looking, octagonal beige and brown tile and a tan deck with white spacers.

Our friend, Roy Howard, did the pool's electrical and plumbing work. Later we had a Polynesian hut, or Samoan fale (pronounced FAH-lay), built on the far side of the pool. Under its thatched roof, we played many games of table tennis, while those not playing splashed and enjoyed swimming on Sacramento's often terrifically hot summer days. Diving or doing "preacher's seats" off the white diving board into the blue water was a favorite sport of the boys and their friends. On the hottest of the summer Sabbaths, when temperatures could top out at 115 degrees, we allowed "quiet swims," so the boys could cool off a bit.

Many birthday parties were held on the back patio by the pool, as well, with cake and ice cream served on the picnic table. An almond tree grew out of an opening left in the cement by the original builder, giving shade to the area.

Big sliding glass doors led from both the living room and dining room onto the patio. A set of clippers was kept in a dining room cupboard, and on summer days, haircuts were given to the recorded sounds of Roger Whitaker, the Beach Boys, and other singers and musicians. The boys and Dean never had commercial haircuts during all those years and, of course, the budget benefitted.

A music teacher had built the home in 1959. The second owners were Ivan Tinder and his mother, Viola. We bought it from them in 1973 for $50,000—a big budget stretch for us, just finishing school, but Dean had a good job as a principal, and we felt we could handle the $301 monthly payment and, of course, we did. The original price was $65,000, but the Tinders loved the idea of five boys being raised there, and they told us they were lowering the price to help us out (and no doubt to get the place sold).

Glenn and Martha Gum lived to the west in an old, farm style home, and Carol Anderson, a widow lady, lived to the east. Our place was private, and quiet, and considered safe because thieves had no quick getaway and were unlikely to try anything.

To this point in our family life, we had not had a dog or a cat, though the boys had often asked for one. Either animals had not been allowed in our university rental homes, or it simply was not convenient to have a pet, However, we decided this was definitely the right time to have this experience.

When we first moved into the house, we all went for a ride one day in the country, and our oldest son Glenn, age eleven, spotted a sign that said, "Free German Shepherd Puppies." How could we resist? We pulled into the farmhouse driveway, and Glenn was the first out of the car and the one who ran straight to a darling pup, a shy little female. He scooped her up in his arms and ran back to our VW Van as his father and I talked with the owner.

Originally one of the boys had said, "Let's drive in and see what the pups look like." This, of course, quickly developed into, "Let's get this one, Dad," and so we did. It turned out the pup was a mixed breed, a Collie/German Shepherd, with pretty black/brown markings, floppy ears, and soft, brown eyes.

We named her Lady, and she was an important part of our lives for the next 13 years, a gentle, loving dog who warmed our hearts. We all remember her lying by the fireplace, barking to warn us of visitors or intruding animals, and sleeping by the boys on summer nights in the back yard, curled up beside them in their sleeping bags.

Like a sentinel, Lady would leave her bed in the ivy beneath the kitchen window every afternoon about three o'clock. She would trot to the swale in the driveway and lie there, unerring in knowing when the first boy was due to arrive. Tail wagging, she would run to meet each boy as he turned in by the mailbox.

Lady had her own way of saying "Goodbye" to the boys each morning when they left for school, and so did I. As a stay-at-home mom, it became a daily ritual, that as the boys would leave, she would stand very still on the porch and look quite forlorn while I, meanwhile, would wave to them from the kitchen window until they were out of sight.

When Lady grew older, her gait slowed, but her faithfulness never failed. Parting from her when she was 13 years old was like losing a member of the family. We all remember her with such fondness and love. She was such a loyal, loveable dog with brown eyes that melted our hearts.

Before our move to Idaho in 1985, Lady's health rapidly declined, and we had to put her to sleep. Greg and our dear friend, Vickie Brown, went with her to the vet's, and the rest of us each said "Goodbye" in our own way to a faithful friend who had brought much joy and happiness to all of us.

In addition to our dear dog Lady who meant so much to all of us, we also acquired a beautiful boxer we named Buddy. Barry was especially fond of this kind and gentle dog. He was an old dog that just appeared one day, and we couldn't resist adopting him.

Lady was a bit out of sorts for a while, but she adjusted. Buddy, however, didn't stay with us very long. He disappeared one day as quickly as he had become part of our family. We all missed him.

Another of our animals was a darling, black and white kitty Greg and his dad found while they were on an afternoon trip to the foothill village of Fiddletown, near Placerville. Appropriately, Greg named his new, little treasure Fiddle. When all of us went on a family trip back East, Fiddle disappeared, Greg remained sad for a long time, and Mama was sad because her little guy was so forlorn.

Our menagerie came to include cows, horses, pigs, sheep, goats, Barry's pet rats, and a few cats. Our animals, through the care they needed, taught our boys much about responsibility and about the cycle of life and death.

Each of the boys remember so much about the home.

Barry, for example, built his famous "fort" on Gum's side of the house. It was actually a huge pit he could crawl into. At one point, he also buried the remains of an old car on that same side of the house.

Glenn, meanwhile, as the oldest teenager, used the back pasture to "run away from home" a time or two. He would take his sleeping bag and leave the house in a fit only to return and rejoin us a few hours later. I suppose we all need to run away now and again to realize how good we have it where we are.

The back lawn sloped down toward the entrance to the pasture and then rose again to the back line of the property. The boys mowed the big lawn for twelve years without complaint. It was just part of the many chores required to keep things looking their best.

When we bought the home, the exterior was an ugly, dark green, and the place quite run down. We set about replacing the paint with a much lighter shade of green, and our dear friend, Nephi Levin, made some attractive shutters and decorative kitchen window trim to grace the front. These improvements and the long, white fence made the approach to the home quite lovely.

A low brick wall in front rimmed the rock garden, and we replaced the old, uneven brick walkway leading to the front door with crushed aggregate set in cement. This proved to be both solid and safe, as well as attractive.

A second walkway with three steps approached the house from the paved area where we parked the cars, and this was the one we used most of the time. Under the upstairs window, we also put in a basketball hoop which saw its share of use by all our boys and their friends.

From the front porch, a heavy door with an equally heavy, fancy, burnished brass lock gave access to the home's entry way. To the right of the door was a narrow, louvered window. We sometimes moved the unscreened louvers to get in when a key was forgotten.

Stepping up into the house, the view from the big glass doors of the living room was stunning—looking out over the marine blue water of the pool, the Polynesian hut, and the many varieties of trees and shrubs in the pasture. Perhaps it was this view (even *without* the pool and hut then in place) that first sold us on the house—or perhaps it was the spirit of the place that made it seem so right for us.

The living room, a gracious room, featured a decorative white brick fireplace with fluted wood trim which we also painted white. We installed a wood-burning stove, mostly for supplementary emergency heating and cooking.

Turning right from the front entry was a long hallway with two roomy coat closets on either side and, at the end of the hall, four large linen closets with two pull-out utility boards.

Mom's and Dad's bedroom faced the front of the house, and Dad's office, with it's hardwood floors, brown and green woven wood blinds, and ceiling fan was to the right of the bedroom. The blue bedroom at the rear of the house was set aside for baby Greg (18 months) and Robbie (age three).

A roomy, green-tile bathroom served this end of the house, with fleur de lis wallpaper and drawer handles, double green sinks, a green bathtub, and separate stall shower. Aunt Mary later helped replace the original wallpaper with flocked green flowers on a white background, and Mom said it made her feel like being in a garden.

We also added country-style wallpaper to the long, parallel wall kitchen which took off to the left of the front door. This huge kitchen seemed to have endless cabinet space and a unique, one-of-a-kind sink surrounded by a beige and brown tile counter top. From it you could look out through the sliding glass doors of the formal dining room window, out to the back yard, and on to the pasture.

After ten years in the home, we remodeled the small bath off the laundry room and put some new, seafoam green carpet and pretty matching floral wallpaper in the dining room. The dining room also housed some blond wood bookcases and shelves where we kept a goodly supply of books and records. We had many Sunday family dinners in this room.

A wall oven marked the far end of the kitchen, and a range sat mid-way between the two front windows. Near the smaller of the windows was our grain mill, and it fell to Greg to be the official family miller.

Commercial cereal was too expensive to use on a daily basis, so we ground our own wheat, which served seven of us breakfast for a total of a nickel. This same cost savings was still amazingly in place 30 years later because wheat prices remained stable. We also made our own tasty whole wheat pancakes and waffles, serving commercial cereals only on Sundays for a treat.

It was in the kitchen that Greg, as a little boy, often said how much he liked seeing Dad give Mom a kiss and a hug, usually as she was busy at the sink. Greg became known as "the magnet," because, when he saw this kind of affection, he would immediately run to both of us, position his little self as close between us as he could, and put his arms around our legs—just as if he were drawn there by a magnet.

When the boys were all in school, we had a nightly ritual of making five sack lunches. We bought natural peanut butter in 30-pound tubs, and the boys never seemed to tire of peanut butter and jelly sandwiches with fruit, vegies, and a little treat of some kind. We often included a love note to remind them of parents who cared so very much for them and prayed they would always be guided and protected.

It was common for a vocal prayer to be offered, often at the front door, as the boys left for school. A regret was that we all did not rise a little earlier, have scripture study together, and kneel for prayer each day. This had not been an occurrence in either Dean's or my home, and it seemed hard for us to develop this important habit. We did, however, hold our Family Home Evenings regularly each Monday night, and we did enjoy reading to the boys. A favorite book we all read together in our living room was **Where the Red Fern Grows**. I believe there wasn't a dry eye when we finished that wonderful story.

We limited television almost exclusively to the weekends and then carefully monitored what the boys were watching. Week nights were for homework.

Our kitchen breakfast nook became the family gathering place, and the picnic table there served as a setting for thousands of family meals and also as a learning center. Homework was often done on that table, as well as memorization of the books of the **Bible**, among other endeavors. A wall calendar posted all our many comings and goings, and on the opposite wall we mounted a big corkboard to display school papers and art work.

The white, interior window shutters by that well-used kitchen table looked out over the front lawn and pasture, up the driveway and on over to McKinney's home and the gigantic palm tree behind it. Three other large palms graced the front of Gum's home and added a unique California flavor to our view.

Having a limited budget, we furnished this home we loved completely from garage sales and newspaper ads featuring used furniture. Amazingly, we never bought a new piece of furniture while living there. Any extra money we had went to travel. It seemed a much better investment in our boys' lives.

Off the kitchen was our laundry room and a small bathroom with a sink, toilet, and stall shower used mostly by the boys. The laundry room's unfailing G.E. washer and dryer put out two loads of laundry almost every day except Sunday. The ironing board standing open on the opposite wall had five seemingly never-ending piles of folded laundry on it. Figuring 600 loads a year for twelve years, that would be about 7,200 loads. GE did build a fine set of machines to take that kind of work load.

I never minded doing the laundry, but if the boys did not take their pile and put it away, I told them I would toss it on the back patio, and I did that a time or two to remind them of their responsibility. Thinking back, I wonder how I could have been so harsh. However, I didn't want to say something and then not follow through. Dean, meanwhile, taught the boys to all pin their socks at the toe, and this saved hundreds of lost or mis-matched pairs.

Upstairs from the kitchen, and over the big garage, were two huge bedrooms. We would all swing around from the kitchen onto the first step rather than stepping down to the landing and then up again. Four steps led down to the big double-car garage and a coat rack by the garage door for the boys' jackets on the landing. Nine steps led up to the bedrooms.

Our two oldest, Glenn and Matthew, generally occupied the front room, and the younger boys the back room—with some switching around now and then. From the windows we could look out over the front and rear pastures, and in the mornings this was the best place to hear the roosters crow. Aunt Mary slept up there when she visited and often said she wished she had a shotgun when they started their ruckus. Her annual visits, along with Uncle Ken, were a highlight of the year.

When Robbie and Greg were old enough, Dean surprised me one day by moving them upstairs and setting up an office for me in the blue room. I was happy to have the office, but felt badly to have moved the younger boys, knowing they were no longer babies and could now be away from us and with their older brothers.

Grandma and Grandpa Hoch came several times from Pennsylvania, once bringing Aunt Hazel and Uncle Raymond. Aunt Joyce and Uncle Chuck and others also visited and seemed to enjoy their time with us so much. My mother was too sick to ever make the trip to that home. She and Aunt Barb and Dean's dad all died back in Pennsylvania while we lived there—and all in 1975. Glenn and I flew back to Pennsylvania for my mother's funeral in January of that year. Barb died in March, and Dean and Robbie made the trip for Grandpa's funeral in July.

Many friends also spent time at our home. Ours seemed like a continuously busy household, and I remember saying many times with a big sigh, "It never ends!" But I know now that all our challenges and trials eventually *do* end and that it's so important to focus on the joys instead of the frustrations. The times with our little ones pass all too quickly, and a noisy home filled with children is suddenly silent, echoing only the sounds of the love and laughter that once were there.

A detailed physical description of this home seems important because it was here that seven lives, and assuredly many more, were and will be molded and influenced because of all that occurred in and around that home and the times that were shared there.

We are grateful for so many wonderful people, Scout leaders, teachers, and friends who also were a part of our lives in Fair Oaks. Just a few of the names include the Kloepfers, the Dziedzics, the Beus's, the Woods, the Braggs, the Jones's, the Walmers, and so many, many more.

All of us loved this special home, but probably none of us realized just how much at the time. In some ways this is like the best of relationships within a family. A home, like our relationships, demands attention, hard work and commitment if it is to flourish and be all that it can be. Both a home and relationships with loved ones are often taken for granted. We do not stop to appreciate what we have, but ultimately we come to realize just how precious both our home and, more importantly, our loved ones really are.

After we moved to Idaho, we rented the home for 11 years. Unfortunately, it was neglected by the tenants and not given much in the way of love and caring. After praying for guidance, Dean and I felt it best to sell it in August of 1996—a difficult decision at best. Somehow parting with a home such as this is like parting with a dear friend.

My mother often said a home has its own personality, its own spirit. She maintained that some homes are happy homes and some are not. This, of course, could simply be a reflection of the people who live there. Dean, with a smile, wryly says, "You can't always be dwelling on a dwelling." He's right, of course. It's the family that lives in that home that matters.

Not wanting to look back, still I wish we could have done more to teach important truths and values on a day-to-day basis. However, we all have to look forward, and the hope is that each generation will improve on the one before.

"Going home again" is a bittersweet process. The memories of our lives at 8549 Sunset Avenue seem endless: Just a tiny few include Glenn's winning his sixth grade little league game as the star catcher—and six years later his graduation in 1980 from Bella Vista High School. Another was a call from Matthew's high school P.E. coach; Matt had found a $10 bill on the floor in the locker room and turned it in. The coach said, "What a tribute to him and to your family for such an act of honesty." Barry won the Royal Reader contest and met with a famous author. Robb scared us to death by not arriving at junior high school one day as scheduled (we wondered if he'd been kidnaped), and we remember so well the day we sent our last little one, Greg, off to kindergarten, Mama with tears in her eyes.

So much more could be said about each of the boys and the unbounded love we have for them. The rather lengthy stories of the boys' growing up years that we have written elsewhere for each of them detail much of their growing up years in California.

Their five personalities are so vastly different that people have asked us if they really are from the same parents and family. The amazing thing is how close they have all remained—how supportive they are of each other and how well they still get along together. Even when they were little, they rough housed and bantered back and forth a lot, but they were never mean to each other and didn't fist-fight like many brothers do … at least not that their mother can remember. How grateful we, as parents, are for the love they have for each other.

Barry and Brenda were privileged, along with the two of us, to visit our home one last time before it sold, and Barry offered a warm and sincere prayer as we left this wonderful place. Among other things, he thanked Heavenly Father for being able to come to say "Goodbye to our home," and he gave special thanks for family and friends.

The last part of that prayer has special meaning. If we truly give prayerful thanks for the dear ones who share our lives, then we will be building lasting and rewarding relationships, independent of our immediate physical surroundings—no matter how special those surroundings might be. And isn't that what the best of "going home again" is really all about?

A final thought: Part of the nostalgia of thinking of an earthly home we have loved so much is also thinking of our heavenly home. All of us **will** go home again—to that eternal home we left when we were born into this temporary learning and testing experience here on earth.

This heavenly home is one that will be ours forever. It will never be sold, nor will it fall into disrepair. That home will not be diminished by the negatives and sorrows and pain of life, as we live it, in this telestial sphere. Rather, it will welcome us with all the happy memories now veiled from our mortal eyes. It will be the dearest and best home of all—the mansion promised to us and prepared for us, by our Heavenly Father and his beloved Son, the Savior of the world.

As the British poet, William Wordsworth, wrote so beautifully in his thought-provoking poem, "Intimations of Immortality" …

Our birth is but a sleep and a forgetting:
The Soul that rises with us, our life's Star,
Hath had elsewhere its setting,
And cometh from afar;
Not in entire forgetfulness,
And not in utter nakedness,
But trailing clouds of glory do we come
From *God*, who is our *home*.

WAVING GOODBYE

It has always been hard for me to wave "Goodbye"—sometimes even to simply *say* "Goodbye."

When I was five, my older sister took me to see "Snow White and the Seven Dwarfs." At the end of the film, everyone in the theater was happy to see Snow White ride off with the prince. Only little Nancy was crying. My sister said, "What's the matter, honey?" And I replied, as I sobbed, "I didn't want Snow White to leave the seven dwarfs."

And so it has gone throughout my life.

I hated leaving high school … choking up at graduation, tears brimming as "Pomp and Circumstance" filled the air.

Leaving my parents in Pennsylvania after Dean and I were married, and we left for our new home in California, was a difficult time.

As our boys grew, I hated the day each of them left for kindergarten—especially the first and the last ones, knowing what a big transition this was in their lives and in mine.

Deaths of dear ones have taken their toll.

As to the day-to-day farewells, as the boys grew, our youngest, Greg—perhaps because he was the youngest—seemed to be the most attached to home. Each day, when he reached the top of the driveway and turned to head down the hill, he would look back and wave again and again. This became a game, of sorts, especially when he was very young.

On the road, at the top of the driveway, the hillside sloped downward, and at that point, as Greg began the gradual descent, he would wave again, and I would wave back. Realizing the hill was quickly separating us, he would anxiously wave another time. Then, after another few yards, with only his head showing, he would jump up and wave yet again. Then his head would disappear, and he would jump just high enough for me to catch a glimpse of only the top of his head and his hand. Then he was gone.

Often, with the last wave, my nose would tickle, and tears would brim.

How like life, I realized then—and even more so now. Our children are obviously physically and emotionally very close to us when they are small. As parents, most of us take that closeness totally for granted. However, from the day of their birth, they begin their move toward independence, and the daily transition is deceptively gradual, deluding us into thinking they will somehow always be with us.

However, little by little, major signals come to let us know that this will not be the case—that all-important first day of school, entering junior high, then high school, dating, graduation, and all the little changes that occur in between these landmark events.

Almost without our being aware, they wave for the last time, so to speak, and are suddenly apart from us—independent and grown and gone. We have worked ourselves right out of the most important job in the world.

What can we do while we have them with us but try to be more aware of the importance of each day—the need for an extra word of love and praise, the need to drop everything and read a book with them, go for a walk, pick flowers together, play in the snow, or whatever else might capture a memory?

Ralph Waldo Emerson's quote comes to mind:
"Write it on your heart that every day is the best day in the year."
I might add: Seize not just the day, but the hour, and the minute.
Greg is a man now, as are his brothers, of course. Still, in my mind's eye, I see my youngest turning and waving, turning and waving, turning and "waving goodbye." That simple, little ritual is a memory the two of us will always share.

To this day, we continue to wave at parting until one or the other of us is lost from view.

SPECIAL NOTE: It was remembering these times of waving "Goodbye" to Greg that prompted the title of this book and then the compilation of all the essays.

EPILOGUE

All Too Soon

Inevitably, in all our lives ... and all too soon ... it is time for that final farewell.

After all, we have in essence been preparing for that event ever since we arrived on the planet. Reluctantly, we must wave goodbye for the last time to this beautiful earth with its glorious pageantry of nature, to our family, friends, and all that we hold dear.

Lines from Alfred Lord Tennyson's well-known poem, "Crossing the Bar" provide a rich analogy:

> Sunset and evening star,
> And one clear call for me!
> And may there be no moaning of the bar,
> When I put out to sea,
>
> But such a tide as moving seems asleep,
> Too full for sound and foam,
> When that which drew from out the boundless deep
> Turns again home.
>
> Twilight and evening bell,
> And after that the dark!
> And may there be no sadness of farewell,
> When I embark;
>
> For tho' from out our bourne of Time and Place
> The flood may bear me far,
> I hope to see my Pilot face to face
> When I have crossed the bar.

Our ship must eventually put out to sea, yet inherent in that sailing is the joy of "Saying Hello" to those who have arrived before us on the other shore, and the whole new adventure that awaits us there.

We have simply reversed the process of "Waving Goodbye" and "Saying Hello." Instead of being born on the earth, we wave "Goodbye" to it and "Say Hello" to a whole new world.

With our leaving, we make room for others to have their turn on the playground of life.

To my own posterity, my wish would be that this book of vignettes and essays will help them see the great potential of life on earth, brief though it is at its longest—how life presents to each of them the chance to exercise their agency in choosing the right, doing their best to improve each day, and making the most of the privilege of being here. I am grateful to have had the chance to share my experiences, my thoughts, and my heartfelt feelings about my own turn on earth.

The "Hellos" of each of our lives are only doorways to endless opportunities. The "Goodbyes," though often difficult, are a necessary part of the changing, and learning, and growing, and the possibilities of more endless opportunities.

When I depart this life, sentimentalist that I am, I will leave behind my deepest love and affection with those so dear to me and, with a tear (and a twinkle) in my eye, I will turn and "wave goodbye" one last time—until the day that I wave and "say hello" to them once more.

978-0-595-42018-6
0-595-42018-4